GRANDMA'S KITCHEN

Comfort Cooking from Canadian Grandmas

by Irene Hrechuk
& Verna Zasada

Front Cover: Puffy Oven Pancake with Fresh Fruit, page 26

GRANDMA'S KITCHEN
by
Irene Hrechuk & Verna Zasada

First Printing – June 2003

Published by Publishing Solutions, A Division of PrintWest Communications Ltd.

National Library of Canada Cataloguing in Publication Data

Hrechuk, Irene, 1943 –

Grandma's kitchen : comfort cooking from Canadian grandmas / Irene Hrechuk, Verna Zasada ; Margo Embury, editor.

Includes index.
ISBN 1-894022-86-6

1. Cookery, Canadian.   I. Zasada, Verna, 1934 –   II. Embury, Margo, 1943 – III. Title.

TX715.6.H73 2003   641.5971   C2003-911136-9

Food Photography by
Patricia Holdsworth
Patricia Holdsworth Photography
Regina, Saskatchewan

Formatting and index by
Iona Glabus, Centax Books

Designed, Printed and Produced in Canada by
Centax Books, a Division of PrintWest Communications Ltd.
Publishing Director, Editor, Photo Designer & Food Stylist: Margo Embury
1150 Eighth Avenue, Regina, Saskatchewan, Canada S4R 1C9
(306) 525-2304   FAX: (306) 757-2439
centax@printwest.com   www.centaxbooks.com

TABLE OF CONTENTS

Recipes have been tested in U.S. Standard measurements. Common metric measurements are given as a convenience for those who are more familiar with metric. Recipes have not been tested in metric.

INTRODUCTION

Grandma's Touch, *Grandma's Best* and, now, *Grandma's Kitchen* – authors Irene Hrechuk and Verna Zasada celebrate Canadian cooking as traditional favorites from many other countries become new Canadian traditions. Growing up with the wonderful flavors of Norwegian, British, Ukrainian, Polish and "Canadian" food, they experienced a rich culinary and cultural heritage. Through sharing recipes with new family members, friends and neighbors, they have expanded their repertoire of treasured recipes to reflect Canada's superb multicultural cuisine.

Whatever our culinary heritage, we all have fond memories of the foods we enjoyed as children. Treasured family recipes were part of every special occasion.

Food and hospitality are an important part of our ethnic and personal culture. As we expand our culinary palates to include new dishes, brought to Canada by new Canadians, we also share the hospitality and culture of these new friends.

In *Grandma's Kitchen*, as with their previous cookbooks, Irene and Verna have combined some of their best family recipes with classic recipes that are fast becoming important and delicious staples in Canadian cooking. They have also simplified many of these recipes, and updated them for today's busy health-conscious cooks.

With traditional recipes, the recipes often vary from family to family. In *Grandma's Kitchen*, variations and substitutions are included with many basic recipes. These suggestions make the recipes more versatile and they inspire novice cooks to be creative in adapting new recipes.

Remembering grandma's kitchen always conjures up images of comforting aromas and satisfying flavors. The kitchens of Canadian grandmothers contain memories of some of the best food the world has to offer, from generations of great home cooks. With *Grandma's Kitchen* you can prepare your special childhood favorites as grandma used to make them. You can also prepare some of the fabulous recipes made by your friends' grandmas.

Biscuits, Muffins, Loaves & Breads

Close your eyes and imagine the smell
of baking bread, nothing can compare
with the aroma of grandma's kitchen
on baking day. Homemade biscuits,
muffins and breads hot from the oven
make any meal a feast.

BUTTERMILK BISCUITS

THESE LIGHT, FLUFFY BISCUITS ARE GREAT WITH A BOWL OF HOT SOUP!

3 cups	all-purpose flour	750 mL
1½ tsp.	salt	7 mL
4 tsp.	baking powder	20 mL
½ tsp.	baking soda	2 mL
⅓ cup	vegetable shortening OR butter	75 mL
1½ cups	buttermilk	375 mL

- Sift flour, salt, baking powder and baking soda into a mixing bowl.
- With a pastry blender, cut shortening into dry ingredients.
- Add buttermilk all at once; stir in only until dry ingredients are moistened.
- Turn dough out onto a lightly floured surface. With a minimum of handling, flatten dough to 1" (2.5 cm) thickness. With a floured 2" (5 cm) biscuit cutter, cut out biscuits; place on a parchment-paper-lined baking sheet.
- Let biscuits stand at room temperature for 15 minutes.
- Bake at 350°F (180°C) for 15-20 minutes, or until just lightly browned.

VARIATIONS   Biscuits are infinitely versatile – you may add herbs and cheeses to the dry ingredients; try ¼ cup (60 mL) minced green onion or chives OR 1 tsp. (5 mL) dried Italian seasoning, parsley, rosemary or oregano; try ½ cup (125 mL) grated Parmesan OR up to 1 cup (250 mL) grated sharp Cheddar. Cayenne pepper or minced jalapeño add extra zip with the Cheddar. With the liquid ingredients, you may add up to ½ cup (125 mL) cooked sausage or ham.

YIELD   *16 – 20 BISCUITS*

GOOD OL' PLAIN MUFFINS

A GREAT BASIC WITH TASTY VARIATIONS

1	egg	1
1 cup	milk (room temperature)	250 mL
½ tsp.	vanilla	2 mL
¼ cup	melted butter	60 mL
2 cups	all-purpose flour	500 mL
¼ cup	sugar	60 mL
1 tbsp.	baking powder	15 mL
½ tsp.	salt	2 mL

- In a small mixing bowl, beat together egg, milk, vanilla and butter.
- In a large mixing bowl, thoroughly combine flour, sugar, baking powder and salt.
- Add the liquid mixture to the dry ingredients all at once. Mix just until moistened. The batter should be lumpy.
- Spoon batter into 12 greased medium muffin cups. Bake at 400°F (200°C) for 15-20 minutes, or until lightly golden brown and a toothpick inserted in the center of the muffin comes out clean.
- Place on a cooling rack for 10 minutes; remove muffins from pan.

VARIATIONS *Cranberry Orange Muffins* – Add 1 cup (250 mL) of dried cranberries and 1 tbsp. (15 mL) of grated orange rind to the dry ingredients.

Blueberry or Strawberry Muffins – Gently fold in 1 cup (250 mL) of sliced strawberries or 1 cup (250 mL) of blueberries after wet and dry ingredients have been combined.

Blueberry Lemon Muffins – Also add 2 tbsp. (30 mL) fresh lemon juice and grated zest of 1 lemon. Add to egg mixture.

Buttermilk, Sour Cream or Yogurt Muffins – Add ½ tsp. (2 mL) baking soda to the dry ingredients; substitute 1 cup (250 mL) buttermilk, sour cream or yogurt for the milk.

NOTE Most muffins may be prepared the night before, including filling the pans. Refrigerate overnight, then bake to serve hot for breakfast.

YIELD *12 MEDIUM MUFFINS*

Banana Muffins

FREEZE RIPE BANANAS TO HAVE ON HAND FOR THESE MELLOW MUFFINS

½ cup	butter, softened	125 mL
¾ cup	sugar	175 mL
1	egg	1
½ cup	chopped walnuts (optional)	125 mL
3	ripe bananas, mashed	3
1 tsp.	baking soda	5 mL
1½ cups	all-purpose flour	375 mL
1 tsp.	salt	5 mL
1 tsp.	vanilla	5 mL

- In a large bowl, cream together butter and sugar until light and fluffy. Beat in egg. Stir in walnuts.
- Combine bananas and baking soda. Add to creamed mixture.
- Combine flour and salt. Add to creamed mixture and stir only until just moistened. Stir in vanilla.
- Spoon batter into 12 greased medium muffins cups, filling ¾ full. Bake at 375°F (190°C) for 18 minutes, until tops spring back when touched.

YIELD   *12 MEDIUM MUFFINS*

Bran-Cran Muffins

HIGH-FIBER, HIGH-FLAVOR BREAKFAST MUFFINS

3 cups	natural wheat bran	750 mL
2 cups	whole-wheat flour	500 mL
1 tbsp.	baking powder	15 mL
1 tsp.	baking soda	5 mL
¼ tsp.	salt	1 mL
1 cup	dried cranberries	250 mL
2	eggs, lightly beaten	2
⅓ cup	EACH vegetable oil & liquid honey	75 mL
⅓ cup	blackstrap molasses	75 mL
2 cups	buttermilk	500 mL

BRAN-CRAN MUFFINS
(CONTINUED)

- In a large bowl, combine bran, flour, baking powder, baking soda and salt. Stir in cranberries.
- In a small bowl, combine eggs, oil, honey, molasses and buttermilk.
- Make a well in dry ingredients. Add liquid ingredients all at once; mix only until dry ingredients are moistened.
- Spoon batter into 24 greased medium muffin cups, filling ⅔ full. Bake at 350°F (180°C) for 20-25 minutes, until tops are firm.

YIELD　　　*24 MEDIUM MUFFINS*

RHUBARB OAT MUFFINS
SUPER SNACKING MUFFINS – TANGY AND SWEET

1½ cups	all-purpose flour	375 mL
1 tsp.	EACH baking soda & baking powder	5 mL
½ tsp.	salt	2 mL
1 cup	quick oats	250 mL
¾ cup	brown sugar	175 mL
2 tbsp.	vegetable oil	30 mL
2	eggs	2
2 tsp.	vanilla	10 mL
1½ cups	finely diced rhubarb	375 mL
¾ cup	buttermilk	175 mL
½ cup	chopped pecans (optional)	125 mL
1 tbsp.	brown sugar	15 mL
1 tsp.	cinnamon	5 mL

- Sift flour, baking soda, baking powder and salt into a small mixing bowl. Stir in oats and set aside.
- In a larger bowl, combine brown sugar, oil, eggs and vanilla. Mix well. Stir in rhubarb, buttermilk, and pecans.
- Add dry ingredients and mix just until moistened. Spoon batter into 12 greased medium muffin cups, filling ⅔ full.
- Combine brown sugar and cinnamon and sprinkle evenly on muffins. Bake at 425°F (220°C) for 20 minutes.

YIELD　　　*12 MEDIUM MUFFINS*

MULTI-GRAIN MUFFINS

SPICY LOW-FAT MUFFINS WITH A CRUNCHY TEXTURE — APPLESAUCE REPLACES
SOME OF THE OIL AND MAKES THESE MUFFINS MOIST AND FLAVORFUL

1¼ cups	all-purpose flour	300 mL
1 cup	multi-grain cereal	250 mL
½ tsp.	salt	2 mL
½ tsp.	cinnamon	2 mL
¼ tsp.	nutmeg	1 mL
½ cup	raisins	125 mL
1 cup	buttermilk	250 mL
1 tsp.	baking soda	5 mL
1 tbsp.	vegetable oil	15 mL
½ cup	unsweetened applesauce	125 mL
1	egg	1
¼ cup	brown sugar	60 mL

- In a small bowl, combine flour, cereal, salt, cinnamon, nutmeg and raisins.
- In a large bowl, combine buttermilk and baking soda. Add the remaining ingredients and mix well.
- Add dry ingredients to buttermilk mixture. Mix only until blended.
- Spoon batter into 12 lightly greased medium muffin cups, filling ⅔ full. Bake at 375°F (190°C) for 22 minutes, or until muffins spring back when lightly touched.
- Place on a cooling rack for 5 minutes; remove from muffin pan. Cool completely.

NOTE The 4 oz. (111 g) unsweetened apple fruit snacks measure ½ cup (125 mL). These are convenient to have on hand for baking purposes.

YIELD **12 MEDIUM MUFFINS**

BANANA BREAD

THE CLASSIC WITH A WHOLE-WHEAT TWIST

½ cup	butter, softened	125 mL
1 cup	liquid honey	250 mL
2	eggs	2
3	ripe bananas, mashed	3
1 cup	whole-wheat flour	250 mL
1 cup	all-purpose flour	250 mL
½ tsp.	salt	2 mL
1 tsp.	baking soda	5 mL

- In a small bowl, combine butter, honey and eggs. Blend in bananas.
- In a large bowl, combine the remaining ingredients. Make a well in dry ingredients and add banana mixture. Stir until well blended.
- Pour batter into a greased 5 x 9" (13 x 23 cm) loaf pan. Bake at 350°F (180°C) for 50 minutes, or until center springs back when touched.

VARIATIONS For **Blueberry Banana Bread**, stir 1½ cups (375 mL) fresh blueberries into batter just before pouring batter into prepared pan.
For **Pecan Banana Bread**, stir ⅔ cup (150 mL) coarsely chopped pecans into batter.

YIELD *1 LOAF*

 Bananas are picked green – their flavor develops best when they ripen off the tree. They are high in potassium and vitamin C, also in carbohydrates. Brush peeled, sliced bananas with lemon juice to prevent discoloration.

STRAWBERRY STREUSEL COFFEE CAKE

DELICIOUS WITH STRAWBERRIES, OR TRY BLUEBERRIES AND/OR RASPBERRIES

2¼ cups	all-purpose flour	550 mL
½ cup	sugar	125 mL
⅔ cup	butter, softened	150 mL
½ cup	sliced almonds	125 mL
½ tsp.	EACH baking powder & baking soda	2 mL
¾ cup	milk	175 mL
1 tbsp.	lemon juice	15 mL
1	egg	1
2 tsp.	almond extract	10 mL
2 cups	sliced fresh strawberries	500 mL

- In a large bowl, combine flour and sugar. Cut in butter with a pastry blender until mixture is crumbly. Measure out ½ cup (125 mL); combine in a small bowl with almonds; set aside for streusel topping.
- Add baking powder and baking soda to the large bowl; mix well.
- Combine milk and lemon juice; stir; let sit until thickened, about 5 minutes. Add egg and extract to the thickened milk. Beat well.
- Add liquid mixture to dry ingredients. Stir just until moistened.
- Spread ⅔ of the batter in a greased 10" (25 cm) springform pan about ½" (1 cm) up the sides of the pan to form a shell. Spread sliced strawberries inside shell. Spread remaining ⅓ of batter over strawberries. Sprinkle reserved streusel topping over.
- Bake at 350°F (180°C) for 45-50 minutes.

YIELD   *12 – 16 SERVINGS*

TOFFEE APPLE COFFEE CAKE

RICH FLAVORS COMPLEMENT YOUR MORNING COFFEE

TOFFEE APPLE CAKE:

½ cup	butter, softened	125 mL
1 cup	sugar	250 mL
2	eggs	2
1 tsp.	vanilla	5 mL
2 cups	all-purpose flour	500 mL
1 tsp.	baking powder	5 mL
1 tsp.	baking soda	5 mL
¼ tsp.	salt	1 mL
1 cup	sour cream	250 mL
2	apples, cored, peeled & diced	2
¾ cup	toffee bits	175 mL

TOFFEE, WHITE CHOCOLATE TOPPING:

¼ cup	butter, softened	60 mL
2 tbsp.	brown sugar	30 mL
⅓ cup	all-purpose flour	75 mL
¾ cup	toffee bits	175 mL
½ cup	white chocolate chips	125 mL

- In a large bowl, cream butter and sugar. Add eggs and vanilla; beat well.
- In a small bowl, sift flour, baking powder, baking soda and salt. Add to creamed mixture alternately with sour cream.
- Fold in apples and toffee bits.
- Spread batter evenly in a lightly greased 10 x 15" (25 x 38 cm) jelly roll pan. Combine topping ingredients. Sprinkle over base.
- Bake at 350°F (180°C) for 25 minutes, or until golden brown.

YIELD   12 – 16 SERVINGS

PANETTONE

ITALIAN CHRISTMAS BREAD FROM MILAN – DELICIOUS YEAR ROUND

1 cup	warm water	250 mL
½ cup	sugar	125 mL
2 tsp.	salt	10 mL
½ cup	butter, softened	125 mL
3	eggs	3
1	egg yolk	1
3 cups	all-purpose flour	750 mL
2 tbsp.	instant yeast	30 mL
1 cup	chopped diced citron	250 mL
½ cup	sliced candied cherries	125 mL
1 cup	EACH golden raisins & pine nuts	250 mL
2 tsp.	anise seed	10 mL
1 tsp.	anise extract	5 mL
2½-3 cups	all-purpose flour	625-750 mL
1	egg white	1
2 tbsp.	water	30 mL

- In an electric mixer, with a dough hook, briefly mix water, sugar, salt, butter, eggs, egg yolk and 3 cups (750 mL) of flour.
- While continuing to mix, sprinkle with the yeast. Add citron, cherries, raisins, pine nuts, anise seed and anise extract; mix.
- Gradually add remaining flour until dough comes away from the sides of the bowl and forms a soft dough. In mixer, knead for 5 minutes, or until smooth and elastic.
- Place dough in a lightly greased large bowl. Cover with plastic wrap and let rise in a draft-free area until doubled in volume, about 2 hours. (Fruited dough requires a longer rising time.)
- Transfer dough to a lightly oiled work surface. Divide in half and form into round loaves. Place loaves into 2 greased 7 or 8" (18 or 20 cm) deep round pans. Cover and let rise again until doubled in volume.
- Combine egg white and water, brush over tops of loaves. Bake at 350°F (180°C) for 30 minutes, or until golden brown. Remove loaves from pans and cool on a wire rack.

YIELD   **2 ROUND LOAVES**

JULEKAKE

SCANDINAVIAN CHRISTMAS BREAD FILLED WITH FRUIT AND FRAGRANT WITH CARDAMOM – GREAT ANY TIME OF THE YEAR.

2 cups	all-purpose flour	500 mL
½ cup	sugar	125 mL
1 tsp.	salt	5 mL
1 tsp.	ground cardamom	5 mL
½ tsp.	cinnamon	2 mL
1 cup	milk	250 mL
½ cup	water	125 mL
⅔ cup	butter	150 mL
3	eggs	3
2 tbsp.	instant yeast	30 mL
3½-4 cups	all-purpose flour	825 mL-1 L
½ cup	EACH candied green & red cherries, halved	125 mL
½ cup	raisins	125 mL

- In an electric mixer, with a dough hook, combine 2 cups (500 mL) flour, sugar, salt, cardamom and cinnamon.
- In a small pan, combine milk, water and butter; heat to 120-130°F (49-54°C). Add to flour mixture with eggs. Beat on low until moistened. Sprinkle with yeast while continuing to mix.
- Gradually add remaining flour until dough comes away from the sides of the bowl and forms a soft dough. In mixer, knead for 5 minutes or until smooth and elastic. Knead in cherries and raisins.
- Place dough in a greased bowl; cover loosely with plastic wrap. Let rise in a warm place until doubled in volume, about 40 minutes.
- Punch down dough. Divide into 3 portions; form loaves. Place loaves in lightly greased loaf pans. Cover; let rise until doubled.
- Bake at 350°F (180°C) for 30 minutes, until loaves are golden brown. Cool on wire racks for 5 minutes before removing from pans. Cool completely.
- If desired, drizzle with Vanilla Glaze, page 17.

YIELD   **3 LOAVES**

Cinnamon Buns

Just like Grandma's!

1 cup	water	250 mL
½ cup	milk	125 mL
¼ cup	butter OR margarine	60 mL
½ cup	sugar	125 mL
2 tsp.	salt	10 mL
2	eggs, beaten	2
2 cups	all-purpose flour	500 mL
2 tbsp.	instant yeast	30 mL
3-4 cups	all-purpose flour	750 mL-1L

Cinnamon Raisin Filling:

¼ cup	butter, melted	60 mL
1 cup	brown sugar	250 mL
1 tbsp.	cinnamon	15 mL
1 cup	seedless raisins	250 mL

- In a small saucepan, combine water, milk and butter. Heat to 120-130°F (49-54°C).
- In an electric mixer, with a dough hook, combine water mixture, sugar, salt, eggs and 2 cups (500 mL) of flour.
- While mixing at low speed, sprinkle with yeast. Gradually add remaining flour until dough comes away from the sides of the bowl and forms a smooth elastic ball. In mixer, knead for 5 minutes.
- Transfer dough to a lightly greased bowl. Cover and let rise in a warm place until doubled in volume, about 40 minutes.
- Punch down dough. Turn out onto a lightly oiled board. Divide dough in half.
- Roll 1 half into a rectangle, approximately 10 x 18" (25 x 45 cm). Brush with half the butter.
- Combine brown sugar and cinnamon; sprinkle half over rolled out dough. Sprinkle with half the raisins. Roll up as for a jelly roll, working from the long side. Seal edges firmly. Cut each roll in half; then those halves in half again, resulting in 4 equal pieces. Cut each piece evenly into 3.

CINNAMON BUNS
(CONTINUED)

- Place the 12 pieces in a lightly greased 9 x 13 x 2" (23 x 33 x 5 cm) pan.
- Repeat the process with the other half of the dough.
- Cover and let rise in a warm place until doubled in volume, about 40 minutes.
- Bake at 350°F (180°C) for about 15 minutes, or until golden brown. Cool pans on wire racks for a few minutes. Remove buns to rack to cool completely.
- Serve plain or frost with Vanilla Glaze, see below, or Cream Cheese Frosting, see page 174.

YIELD   *2 DOZEN CINNAMON BUNS*

VANILLA GLAZE
THINNER AND MORE TRANSLUCENT THAN A FROSTING,
THIS GLAZE MAY ALSO BE THINNED FOR BUNDT OR LOAF CAKES

1 cup	icing (confectioner's) sugar	250 mL
¼ tsp.	vanilla	1 mL
3-4 tsp.	milk	15-20 mL

- Combine all ingredients, adding enough milk to obtain desired drizzling consistency. Drizzle over buns, bread or cakes.

VARIATIONS   For a thinner glaze for cakes, increase liquid to 2-3 tbsp. (30-45 mL).

For **Lemon Glaze**, replace milk with fresh lemon juice and add ½ tsp. (5 mL) grated lemon zest.

For a **Coffee** or **Liqueur Glaze**, replace milk with strong coffee, amaretto, Grand Marnier, Irish cream, Kahlúa or your favorite liqueur.

HOT CROSS BUNS

DATING FROM PAGAN TIMES, THESE BUNS BECAME A
CHRISTIAN TRADITION IN MEDIEVAL ENGLAND

1½ cups	milk, scalded	375 mL
½ cup	sugar	125 mL
1 tsp.	salt	5 mL
½ cup	butter	125 mL
2 tbsp.	active dry yeast (2 envelopes)	30 mL
1 cup	lukewarm water	250 mL
2 tsp.	sugar	10 mL
1	egg, beaten	1
1	egg yolk, beaten	1
2 tsp.	EACH cinnamon & cloves	10 mL
1 tsp.	allspice	5 mL
¼ tsp.	nutmeg	1 mL
7-8 cups	all-purpose flour, divided	1.75-2L
1 cup	currants	250 mL
⅔ cup	candied citron	150 mL
1	egg white, slightly beaten	1
1 tbsp.	water	15 mL

- In a large bowl, combine milk with sugar, salt and butter. Stir until butter is melted. Cool to lukewarm.
- In a small bowl, combine yeast, water and sugar; let stand for 10 minutes.
- Stir yeast mixture; add to milk with egg, egg yolk and spices.
- Add 3 cups (750 mL) flour; beat until smooth. Work in remaining flour.
- Turn dough onto a lightly floured surface; knead until smooth and elastic, about 8 to 10 minutes. Knead in currants and citron.
- Shape dough into a smooth ball and place in a greased bowl. Cover loosely; let rise until doubled, about 1½ hours at 80°F (27°C).
- Punch down dough. Shape into 30-36 buns; arrange 2" (5 cm) apart on greased baking sheets and let rise until doubled, about 1 hour.
- Combine egg white and water and brush onto buns. Slash the top of each bun to form a cross. Bake at 350°F (180°C) for 15 to 20 minutes.
- Fill crosses with Vanilla Glaze, see page 17.

YIELD   *3 DOZEN BUNS*

FOCACCIA

FLAVORFUL TOPPINGS CROWN THIS DELICIOUS ITALIAN FLATBREAD

1¼ cups	milk, scalded	300 mL
¼ cup	sugar	60 mL
2 tsp.	salt	10 mL
⅓ cup	olive oil	75 mL
1 tsp.	sugar	5 mL
½ cup	warm water	125 mL
1 tbsp.	active dry yeast (1 envelope)	15 mL
1	egg	1
3-3½ cups	all-purpose flour	750-875 mL
1 tbsp.	EACH onion & garlic powders	15 mL
1 tbsp.	dry Italian seasoning	15 mL
	olive oil	
	additional dry Italian seasoning	
	coarse salt	

- In a large bowl, combine milk, sugar, salt and olive oil. Let cool.
- Dissolve 1 tsp. (5 mL) sugar in warm water. Sprinkle yeast over water and let sit for 10 minutes.
- Beat egg into milk mixture. Add 1 cup (250 mL) of flour; beat on high speed until well blended. Add yeast mixture; beat for 2 minutes. Add 1 cup (250 mL) of flour; beat for 5 minutes, or until smooth.
- In a small bowl, combine the third cup of flour with onion and garlic powders and Italian seasoning. Mix into dough until blended and smooth. Knead in some or all of the remaining ½ cup (125 mL) of flour, only until the dough is smooth and elastic.
- Cover bowl with plastic wrap and a tea towel; let rise in a warm place until doubled in volume. With oiled fingers, spread dough in a well-greased 12 x 12" (30 x 30 cm) baking pan. Let rise for 1 hour.
- Brush with olive oil. Sprinkle with Italian seasoning and coarse salt.
- Bake at 400°F (200°C) for 15-20 minutes, or until golden brown.
- Serve warm or cool.

YIELD   1 LOAF

See photograph on page 67.

TRADITIONAL FRENCH BREAD

CRISP CRUST AND MOIST CHEWY CENTER — HEAVENLY!

3 cups	all-purpose flour	750 mL
2 cups	warm water	500 mL
1 tbsp.	sugar	15 mL
1 tsp.	salt	5 mL
2 tbsp.	vegetable oil	30 mL
2 tbsp.	instant yeast	30 mL
2-2½ cups	all-purpose flour	500-625 mL
	cornmeal	
	water	

- In an electric mixer, with a dough hook, combine flour, water, sugar, salt and oil. Mix in yeast. Gradually add remaining flour until the dough comes away from the sides of the bowl. Knead for 8-9 minutes, or until the dough is smooth and pliable.
- Shape dough into a ball and place in a large well-greased bowl. Cover and let rise in a warm place until doubled in volume, about 30 minutes.
- Turn dough out onto a greased surface, divide in half and form into 2 loaves. Place loaves into a greased and cornmeal-sprinkled 2-loaf French loaf pan (or 2 large baking pans). Make 4-5 diagonal slashes along top of loaves. Let rise until doubled.
- Mist loaves with water. Bake on the middle rack at 375°F (190°C) with a pan of water on the lower rack. After baking for 10 minutes, mist again with water and continue to bake until golden brown. Baked loaves should sound hollow when tapped.

YIELD   *2 LOAVES*

Slashing the tops of loaves before baking assists in the rising of the dough. Misting loaves while baking creates steam which produces a crisp hard crust. French bread and baguette pans vary, depending on the width of the desired loaves. They look like joined half tubes. Baguette pans are 2-3" (5-8 cm) wide and 15-17" (38-43 cm) long. Very thin loaves are called *ficelles* (strings), and are baked in special pans.

BRAIDED SESAME LOAF

DECORATIVE BRAIDED LOAVES ARE A CHERISHED EUROPEAN TRADITION

1 cup	milk	250 mL
¼ cup	butter	60 mL
1 tbsp.	sugar	15 mL
2 cups	all-purpose flour	500 mL
1½ tsp.	salt	7 mL
2	eggs, beaten	2
2 tsp.	instant yeast	10 mL
1½-2 cups	all-purpose flour	375-500 mL
1 tbsp.	milk	15 mL
2 tbsp.	sesame seeds	30 mL

- Gently heat milk, butter and sugar to melt butter and dissolve sugar.
- In a large bowl, combine milk mixture, 2 cups (500 mL) of flour and salt.
- Set aside 1 tbsp. (15 mL) of beaten egg; add remainder to batter.
- Sprinkle yeast over batter; stir in. Add remaining flour until a soft dough forms. Knead until smooth and elastic.
- Place dough in a greased bowl; cover with plastic wrap and let rise in a warm place until doubled in volume.
- Knead dough for about 2 minutes. Divide into 3 equal pieces. Shape each piece into a rope shape about 10" (25 cm) long.
- Lay dough pieces lengthwise on a greased 10 x 15" (25 x 38 cm) baking pan. Braid dough, pinching ends to seal. Cover with plastic wrap; let rise until doubled in volume.
- Whisk milk into reserved 1 tbsp. (15 mL) of beaten egg. Brush over braid. Sprinkle with sesame seeds.
- Bake at 350°F (180°C) for 20 to 25 minutes, or until golden brown and hollow sounding when tapped on the bottom.

YIELD   *1 LARGE BRAIDED LOAF*

DILLY CHEESE BREAD

FRESH FRAGRANT DILL ADDS WONDERFUL FLAVOR

2 cups	2% creamed cottage cheese	500 mL
1 cup	warm water	250 mL
2 tbsp.	vegetable oil	30 mL
2 tbsp.	sugar	30 mL
2 tbsp.	dried, chopped onion flakes	30 mL
2 tsp.	salt	10 mL
2	eggs, beaten	2
2 tbsp.	chopped, fresh dillweed	30 mL
2 cups	all-purpose flour	500 mL
2 tbsp.	instant yeast	30 mL
3-4 cups	all-purpose flour	750 mL-1 L

- Heat the cottage cheese to lukewarm.
- In an electric mixer, with a dough hook, briefly mix cottage cheese, water, oil, sugar, onion, salt, eggs, dillweed and 2 cups (500 mL) flour.
- While continuing to mix, sprinkle with yeast. Add remaining flour until dough comes away from the sides of the bowl.
- Knead dough for 5-6 minutes, or until smooth and elastic.
- Transfer dough to a lightly greased bowl. Cover with plastic wrap and let rise until doubled in volume.
- Transfer dough to a lightly oiled work surface. Divide dough into 3 portions and form loaves.
- Place loaves into greased 5 x 9" (13 x 23 cm/2 L) bread pans. Cover and let rise again until doubled.
- Bake at 350°F (180°C) for 30 minutes, or until golden brown. Remove loaves from pans and cool on a wire rack.

YIELD   *3 LOAVES*

MULTI-GRAIN & SUNFLOWER SEED BREAD

GREAT TEXTURE MEANS HIGH FIBER

3 cups	all-purpose flour	750 mL
½ cup	quick-cooking oat flakes	125 mL
2 tbsp.	raw sunflower seeds	30 mL
3 cups	warm water	750 mL
2 tbsp.	liquid honey	30 mL
2 tsp.	salt	10 mL
2 tbsp.	butter	30 mL
2 tbsp.	instant yeast	30 mL
1 cup	dark rye flour	250 mL
2-3 cups	whole-wheat bread flour	500-750 mL
	vegetable oil	

- In an electric mixer, with a dough hook, combine 3 cups (750 mL) flour, oat flakes, sunflower seeds, water, honey, salt and butter. Mix in yeast.
- Gradually add remaining flour until dough comes away from the sides of the bowl. Knead for 8-9 minutes, or until dough is smooth and pliable.
- Turn dough out onto an oiled surface, divide into 3 portions and form loaves. Place loaves into greased 5 x 9" (13 x 23 cm/2 L) loaf pans. Let rise in a warm place until doubled in volume.
- Bake at 375°F (190°C) for 20-25 minutes, or until bottoms of loaves are browned and sound hollow when tapped.

YIELD   *3 LOAVES*

See photograph on page 33.

RYE BREAD

A GREAT BASE FOR A GRILLED REUBEN SANDWICH!

1 cup	warm milk	250 mL
1 cup	warm water	250 mL
2 tbsp.	honey	30 mL
2 tbsp.	vegetable oil	30 mL
2 tsp.	salt	10 mL
2 cups	dark rye flour	500 mL
1 tbsp.	wheat gluten	15 mL
1 tbsp.	instant yeast	15 mL
2½-3 cups	all-purpose flour	625-750 mL

- In an electric mixer, with a dough hook, combine milk, water, honey, oil, salt, rye flour and wheat gluten. Mix in yeast.
- Gradually add remaining flour until dough comes away from the sides of the bowl. Knead for 8 minutes, or until dough is smooth and elastic.
- Place dough in a greased bowl. Cover and let rise in a warm place until doubled in volume.
- Turn dough onto an oiled surface; divide into 2 portions and form loaves.
- Place loaves into greased 5 x 9" (13 x 23 cm/2 L) loaf pans. Let rise in a warm place until doubled in volume.
- Bake at 350°F (180°C) for 20 to 25 minutes, or until bottom of loaves are browned and sound hollow when tapped.

NOTE   Rye flour contains less gluten than all-purpose or bread flour, therefore, rye bread will not rise well without additional gluten.

YIELD   ***2 LOAVES***

BREAKFAST, BRUNCH & LUNCH

Nourishing and satisfying, breakfasts in grandma's kitchen are a special occasion. Brunch and lunch dishes, some simple, some sumptuous, are perfect for casual family meals and elegant entertaining.

MUESLI

THIS NUTRITIOUS SWISS INVENTION IS AN UNCOOKED GRANOLA

4 cups	slow oats	1 L
1 cup	whole-bran cereal (All Bran or Bran Buds)	250 mL
1 cup	chopped nuts (walnuts, hazelnuts, pecans)	250 mL
1 cup	dried cranberries	250 mL
1 cup	golden raisins	250 mL

- Combine all ingredients. Store in airtight container for up to 6 weeks.
- To serve, place ½ cup (125 mL) of Muesli into a cereal bowl. Add milk or yogurt; stir and let sit for a few minutes.
- Add fresh fruit if desired.

YIELD   8 CUPS (2 L)

PUFFY OVEN PANCAKE WITH FRESH FRUIT

DUTCH AND GERMAN GRANDMAS GET CREDIT FOR THIS

2	eggs, lightly beaten	2
½ cup	milk	125 mL
¼ tsp.	salt	1 mL
½ cup	flour	125 mL
1 tbsp.	butter	15 mL
3 cups	fresh berries OR chopped fresh fruit sour cream OR yogurt for topping brown sugar for topping	750 mL

- In a small bowl, whisk together eggs, milk, salt and flour.
- Place butter in a 9" (23 cm) pie plate; melt in a 450°F (230°C) oven for 2 minutes, or until butter sizzles. Remove pan from oven; tilt to coat with butter.

Puffy Oven Pancake with Fresh Fruit
(Continued)

- Quickly pour whisked batter into pie plate and return to oven. Bake for 15 minutes. Reduce heat to 350°F (180°C) and bake 10 minutes, or until pancake is puffed and golden brown.
- Spoon fruit over pancake. Serve with sour cream and brown sugar.

YIELD   *4 SERVINGS*

See photograph on front cover.

Baked Apple Pancake
Sensational made simple

¾ cup	pancake mix	175 mL
½ cup	water	125 mL
3	eggs	3
1 tbsp.	sugar	15 mL
⅓ cup	butter OR margarine	75 mL
3	apples, peeled, thinly sliced	3
¼ cup	chopped pecans (optional)	60 mL
½ cup	raisins	125 mL
¼ cup	brown sugar	60 mL
2 tsp.	cinnamon	10 mL

- In a medium bowl, combine pancake mix, water, eggs and sugar. Mix well and set aside.
- Melt butter in a skillet over low-medium heat. Add apples; sauté and stir until tender. Place apples in an ungreased 9 or 10" (23 or 25 cm) pie plate. Sprinkle with pecans and raisins. Pour batter over fruit.
- Combine brown sugar and cinnamon. Sprinkle over batter. Loosely cover pancake with a piece of foil. Bake at 400°F (200°C) for 12-15 minutes, or until pancake is puffed.
- Loosen sides of pancake from pie plate and cut into wedges. Serve warm with warm syrup or whipped cream.

YIELD   *6 SERVINGS*

OVERNIGHT BERRY FRENCH TOAST

A LOVELY MAKE-AHEAD BRUNCH DISH

4 cups	French bread cubes	1 L
4 oz.	cream cheese, cubed	115 g
2 cups	fresh blueberries	500 mL
4	eggs	4
½ cup	milk	125 mL
¼ tsp.	cinnamon	1 mL
¼ cup	maple syrup	60 mL
	blueberry syrup	

- Place bread and cheese cubes in a lightly greased 9" (23 cm) square baking pan. Layer berries over top.
- In a small bowl, beat eggs, milk, cinnamon and maple syrup; pour over berries. Refrigerate overnight.
- Bake, uncovered, at 375°F (190°C) for 45 minutes, or until egg mixture is set.
- Serve warm with blueberry syrup.

VARIATIONS Loose-pack frozen blueberries or any fresh berries (raspberries, strawberries, saskatoons) and a corresponding flavored syrup may be substituted for the fresh blueberries.

NOTE This recipe easily doubles or triples for a greater number of servings. Adjust the pan size accordingly.

YIELD *4 SERVINGS*

 Remarkable flavor, excellent nutrition – blueberries are the best source of antioxidents of all fresh fruits and vegetables. If you want to slow down the free radical aging process, scientists recommend eating ½ cup (125 mL) of blueberries a day. Like cranberries, they also contain condensed tannins that can prevent urinary tract infections.

BANANA NUT FRENCH TOAST

CARAMELIZED BANANA SANDWICHES FOR BREAKFAST – OUTSTANDING!

3	eggs	3
¾ cup	milk	175 mL
1 tbsp.	vanilla	15 mL
¼ tsp.	cinnamon	1 mL
⅛ tsp.	nutmeg	0.5 mL
pinch	salt	pinch
3	firm, ripe bananas, sliced	3
¾ cup	brown sugar	175 mL
¾ cup	coarsely chopped, toasted walnuts	175 mL
6	slices French bread	6
1 tbsp.	butter	15 mL
2 tsp.	vegetable oil	10 mL
2 tsp.	butter	10 mL
	maple syrup	

- In a shallow pan, whisk together the eggs, milk, vanilla, cinnamon, nutmeg and salt.
- In a small bowl, combine banana slices, sugar and nuts. Spread ⅓ of banana nut mixture on 3 slices of bread. Top each with a second slice; press to seal sandwiches.
- Place banana sandwiches in the pan with the milk mixture. Let soak for a few minutes per side to absorb mixture.
- Meanwhile, in a small skillet over low heat, heat remaining banana nut mixture until sugar is melted and bananas are soft. Stir in 1 tbsp. (15 mL) butter. Keep warm.
- In a skillet, heat oil and 2 tsp. (10 mL) butter to medium. Add banana sandwiches and fry for 2-3 minutes per side, until golden brown.
- Cut sandwiches into triangles and top with warm banana nut mixture. Serve with maple syrup.

YIELD   4 SERVINGS

"ALL-IN-ONE" BREAKFAST

HEARTY AND SATISFYING – SERVE WITH FRESH FRUIT

FOR EACH SERVING:

2 slices	smoked ham, maple or pepper flavor	2 slices
½ cup	cooked mashed potatoes	125 mL
1	egg	1
	salt & pepper to taste	
	grated Cheddar cheese (optional)	

- Halve ham slices crosswise; line bottom and sides of a small baking dish.
- Spoon mashed potatoes over ham. Make an indentation in the potatoes. Break egg into the indentation. Sprinkle with salt and pepper.
- Bake at 350°F (180°C) for 20-25 minutes, until egg is cooked. Just prior to removing from oven, sprinkle with grated cheese.
- Place dish on a serving plate with a toasted bagel or multi-grain bread.

YIELD   1 SERVING

See photograph on page 33.

WELSH RAREBIT

RAREBIT OR RABBIT – A QUICK LUNCH, APPETIZER OR SNACK

1 tbsp.	butter	15 mL
1 tbsp.	flour	15 mL
1 cup	beer (lager or pale ale)	250 mL
3 cups	grated old Cheddar cheese	750 mL
½ tsp.	dry mustard	2 mL
1	egg, beaten	1
1 tsp.	Worcestershire sauce	5 mL
¼ tsp.	Tabasco	1 mL
¼ tsp.	curry powder (optional)	1 mL
	pinch of salt	
	toasted whole-wheat OR rye bread	
	sliced tomatoes and/or crisp bacon (optional)	

WELSH RAREBIT

(CONTINUED)

- In a double boiler, over simmering water, melt butter. Whisk in flour. Add beer and whisk until slightly thickened. Add cheese, mustard, egg, Worcestershire sauce, Tabasco, curry powder and salt. Whisk until cheese is melted and sauce is thick and smooth.
- Serve rarebit over toast. If desired, top with tomato and/or bacon.

VARIATION   Add 1 cup (250 mL) chopped, drained canned tomatoes.

YIELD   *4 – 6 SERVINGS*

SPINACH FRITTATA

OPEN-FACED ITALIAN OMELET – LIKE A CRUSTLESS QUICHE – SO FEWER CALORIES

8 oz.	fresh spinach, chopped	250 g
5	eggs	5
¼ cup	milk	60 mL
½ tsp.	salt	2 mL
¼ tsp.	pepper	1 mL
1 tbsp.	vegetable oil	15 mL
½	onion, chopped	½
1	garlic clove, minced	1
4	mushrooms, sliced	4

- Steam spinach until just tender. Drain.
- In a small bowl, whisk eggs with milk, salt and pepper.
- In a 9" (23 cm) ovenproof skillet, heat oil and sauté onion, garlic and mushrooms until tender. Stir in spinach.
- Pour in egg mixture. Cook over medium heat for 5 minutes.
- Bake, uncovered, at 350°F (180°C) for 15 minutes, or until center is set.

YIELD   *3 – 4 SERVINGS*

Asparagus-Ham Bake

Colorful, creamy and scrumptious

12-15	asparagus spears	12-15
1 tbsp.	butter	15 mL
4 oz.	cooked ham, diced	115 g
½	medium onion, chopped	½
½	red pepper, chopped	½
1 cup	creamed cottage cheese	250 mL
4	eggs	4
1 cup	buttermilk	250 mL
⅓ cup	all-purpose flour	75 mL
⅓ cup	grated Parmesan cheese	75 mL
	salt & pepper to taste	
2 oz.	grated Cheddar cheese	55 g

- Break the tough ends off asparagus. Cut asparagus into ½" (1 cm) lengths. Steam for 2 minutes, or until just tender.
- In a skillet, melt butter; sauté ham, onion and pepper until onion is tender.
- In a medium bowl, whisk together cottage cheese, eggs, buttermilk, flour, Parmesan cheese, salt and pepper. Stir in asparagus and ham mixture.
- Pour into a lightly greased 9 or 10" (23 or 25 cm) pie plate.
- Bake at 350°F (180°C) for 40 minutes. Sprinkle with Cheddar cheese.
- Bake an additional 15 minutes, or until a knife inserted in the middle comes out clean. Let sit for 10 minutes before serving.

YIELD   *5 SERVINGS*

BREAKFAST

"All-in-One" Breakfast, page 30
Multi-grain & Sunflower Seed Bread, page 23

SHRIMPWICHES

VERSATILE – ALSO DELICIOUS WITH CRAB, TUNA OR SALMON

4 oz.	can small shrimp, drained	115 g
¾ cup	shredded Cheddar cheese	175 mL
2 tbsp.	mayonnaise	30 mL
1 tsp.	lemon juice	5 mL
½ tsp.	Worcestershire sauce	2 mL
3	whole-wheat hamburger buns, halved	3
	paprika	

- In a small bowl, combine shrimp, cheese, mayonnaise, lemon juice and Worcestershire. Spread evenly on halved buns. Sprinkle with paprika.
- Toast buns on a cookie sheet at 450°F (230°C) until bubbly.

YIELD   *6 OPEN-FACED BUNS*

BROCCOLI-HAM BRUNCH

MAKE AHEAD AND RELAX

8 slices	white bread, cubed	8 slices
½ cup	butter, melted	125 mL
8 oz.	shredded sharp Cheddar cheese	250 g
2 cups	chopped, cooked broccoli	500 mL
2 cups	cubed, cooked ham	500 mL
4	eggs	4
2 cups	milk	500 mL
	salt & pepper to taste	

- In a medium bowl, toss cubed bread with butter.
- In a buttered 9 x 13" (23 x 33 cm) pan, layer ½ bread cubes, ½ cheese, ½ broccoli and all of the ham. Add remaining broccoli, cheese and bread.
- In a small bowl, beat eggs, milk, salt and pepper. Pour over layers. Cover.
- Refrigerate a minimum of 2 hours to overnight.
- Bake, uncovered, at 350°F (180°C) for 1 hour, or until puffy and golden.

YIELD   *6 SERVINGS*

Pizza by the Foot

IMAGINATIVE, VERSATILE AND OH SO EASY

1 tbsp.	vegetable oil	15 mL
1½ lbs.	lean ground beef	750 g
5½ oz.	can tomato paste	156 mL
3 tbsp.	water	45 mL
2 tsp.	crushed, dried oregano	10 mL
1 tsp.	salt	5 mL
½ tsp.	pepper	2 mL
1 loaf	French bread	1 loaf
¼ cup	grated Parmesan cheese	60 mL
10 oz.	can sliced mushrooms, drained	284 mL
1	green OR red pepper, sliced	1
½	onion, sliced	½
8 oz.	mozzarella cheese, grated	225 g

- In a skillet, heat oil and brown beef. Add tomato paste, water, oregano, salt and pepper. Simmer for 5 minutes.
- Cut French loaf in half lengthwise. Spread ground beef mixture evenly over both halves. Sprinkle with Parmesan cheese. Layer mushrooms, pepper and onion on top.
- Broil at 300°F (150°C) for 8 minutes. Remove from oven; top with mozzarella cheese. Return to oven for another 3 minutes, or until cheese is melted. Slice and serve warm.

VARIATIONS   Sliced hot pickled peppers and Cheddar cheese may be substituted for the green pepper and mozzarella. Add pineapple slices if you wish, or tomato slices, even a seafood filling, see the Shrimpwiches on page 35, could be presented like this.

YIELD   **8 SERVINGS**

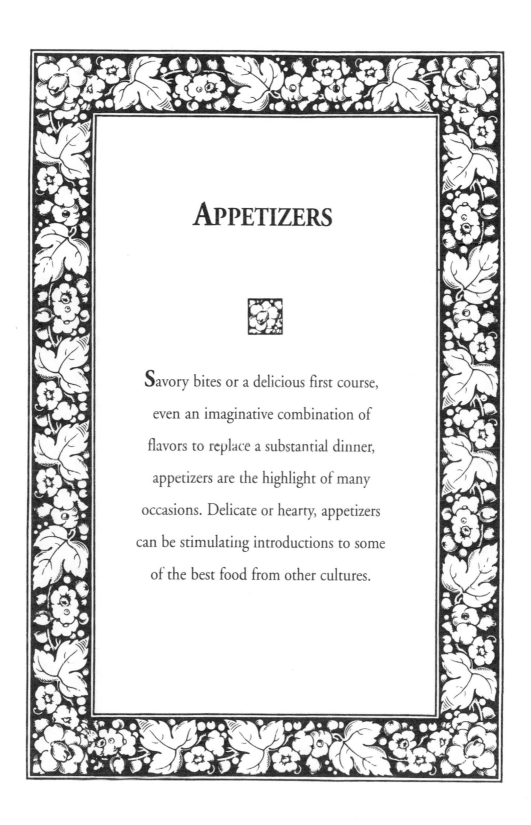

APPETIZERS

Savory bites or a delicious first course,
even an imaginative combination of
flavors to replace a substantial dinner,
appetizers are the highlight of many
occasions. Delicate or hearty, appetizers
can be stimulating introductions to some
of the best food from other cultures.

DEVILED EGGS WITH SIX FILLINGS

GARNISH WITH OLIVE SLICES, PAPRIKA, CRISPY BACON, TINY SHRIMP, PARSLEY, DILL SPRIGS, CHOPPED BASIL OR CHIVES

6	hard-boiled eggs	6
	see filling options below	
4.5 oz.	package alfalfa sprouts (optional)	120 g

- Cut hard-boiled eggs in half lengthwise. Remove yolks.
- In a bowl, mash egg yolks with the chosen filling ingredients.
- Spoon or pipe filling evenly into egg white halves. Garnish.
- For Deviled Eggs in a Nest, arrange on a tray lined with sprouts.

ZESTY CHILI FILLING:

2 tbsp.	mayonnaise	30 mL
2 tbsp.	chili sauce OR hot ketchup	30 mL
1 tsp.	vinegar OR lemon juice	5 mL
½ tsp.	prepared mustard	2 mL
	salt & pepper to taste	

PIMIENTO PICKLE FILLING:

1 tbsp.	finely chopped celery	15 mL
1 tbsp.	chopped pimiento	15 mL
1 tbsp.	sweet pickle relish	15 mL
1 tbsp.	mayonnaise	15 mL
½ tsp.	prepared mustard	2 mL
	salt & pepper to taste	

DILL & CAPER FILLING:

2 tbsp.	EACH sour cream & mayonnaise	30 mL
1½ tsp.	lemon juice	7 mL
¼ tsp.	dry mustard powder	1 mL
2 tbsp.	finely chopped green onion	30 mL
4 tsp.	drained capers	20 mL
1 tsp.	minced fresh dillweed OR tarragon	5 mL
	salt & pepper to taste	
¼ tsp.	Tabasco	1 mL

DEVILED EGGS
(CONTINUED)

ANCHOVY BASIL FILLING:

2 tbsp.	mayonnaise	30 mL
½ tsp.	grainy mustard	2 mL
1 tsp.	cider vinegar	5 mL
¼ tsp.	Worcestershire sauce	1 mL
1½ tsp.	minced basil	7 mL
7	anchovy fillets, minced	7
	salt & pepper to taste	

NIÇOISE TUNA, SHRIMP, CRAB OR LOBSTER FILLING:

2 tbsp.	mayonnaise	30 mL
½ tsp.	Dijon mustard	2 mL
1 tsp.	caper juice OR vinegar	5 mL
6 tbsp.	minced canned tuna, shrimp, crab meat OR lobster	90 mL
2 tsp.	minced chives	10 mL
1 tbsp.	capers	15 mL
	salt & pepper to taste	

HUMMUS FILLING:

1 cup	canned chickpeas	250 mL
2 tbsp.	chopped parsley	30 mL
1 tbsp.	Dijon mustard	15 mL
1	garlic clove, minced	1
1 tbsp.	EACH minced onion & capers	15 mL
1 tbsp.	lemon juice	15 mL
¼ tsp.	Tabasco	1 mL
	salt & pepper to taste	

• Purée all ingredients in a food processor. Add to mashed egg yolks.

NOTE   Leftover filling is delicious on squares of pumpernickel or dark rye bread.

YIELD   ***12 DEVILED EGGS***

SALMON MOUSSE

SILKY SMOOTH – USE SOCKEYE SALMON FOR BEST COLOR AND FLAVOR

2 x 7.5 oz.	cans of salmon	2 x 213 g
13½ oz.	can evaporated milk OR light cream	385 mL
2 tbsp.	unflavored gelatin (2 envelopes)	30 mL
½ cup	mayonnaise	125 mL
⅓ cup	lemon juice	75 mL
⅓ cup	sliced green onions	75 mL
¼ cup	parsley sprigs	60 mL
	salt & pepper to taste	

- Drain salmon, reserving liquid. Discard skin; flake salmon; set aside.
- In a saucepan, combine ⅓ cup (75 mL) of reserved salmon liquid and evaporated milk. Sprinkle gelatin over. Let stand for 10 minutes to soften. Cook over low heat, stirring until gelatin is dissolved. Cool.
- In a food processor, combine gelatin mixture, salmon, mayonnaise, lemon juice, onion, parsley, salt and pepper. Process until smooth.
- Pour the mousse into a 6-cup (1.5 L) loaf pan, terrine or fluted mold. Chill until set. Unmold.
- Serve with crackers, baguette slices or cucumber rounds.

YIELD   *20 APPETIZER SERVINGS*

GLAZED PÂTÉ OLIVE MOLD

IMPRESSIVE BUT SO SIMPLE TO MAKE

8 oz.	liver sausage (pepper, herb OR cognac)	250 g
4 oz.	cream cheese, softened	115 g
3 tbsp.	finely minced onion	45 mL
½ tsp.	Worcestershire sauce	2 mL
10 oz.	can consommé OR beef broth	284 mL
1 tbsp.	unflavored gelatin (1 envelope)	15 mL
10	stuffed olives, halved	10

Glazed Pâté Olive Mold
(Continued)

- In a small bowl, mash sausage, cheese, onion and Worcestershire sauce.
- In a small saucepan, combine consommé and gelatin. Heat to dissolve gelatin. Pour half of consommé mixture into a 4-cup (1 L) pâté mold lined with plastic wrap. Chill. When partially set, arrange olive halves in a row, gently pushing them into the consommé. Chill until set.
- Spread cream cheese mixture over set consommé. Pour remaining consommé over. Chill until set.
- Unmold; garnish and serve with baguette slices, crackers or crudités.

YIELD   20 APPETIZER SERVINGS

Wheat Berry Caviar
A Canadian cousin to tapenade

2-3	garlic cloves	2-3
1 cup	pitted black Greek or Italian olives	250 mL
¼ tsp.	salt	1 mL
½ tsp.	Dijon mustard	2 mL
¼ cup	olive oil	60 mL
1½ cups	precooked wheat berries, see below	375 mL
	chopped parsley & chives for garnish	

- In a food processor, mince garlic cloves. Add olives, salt, mustard and oil; process only until olives are finely minced.
- In a small bowl, toss olive mixture with wheat berries. Garnish and serve with toasted baguette slices or crackers.

YIELD   2 CUPS (500 ML)

To cook hard wheat berries, place 1 cup (250 mL) wheat kernels (berries) and 2 cups (500 mL) water in a small saucepan, bring to a boil. Reduce heat and simmer for 45-60 minutes. The texture will be somewhat crunchy or chewy. Wheat berries may be prepared and used like rice or other grains. They may be topped with chili or stew or stir-fried vegetables. They may be cooked with half water and half apple juice, sprinkled with cinnamon and drizzled with maple syrup for a breakfast treat. Plain yogurt or ricotta and chopped apricots may also be added.

HUMMUS

THIS CLASSIC MIDDLE EASTERN APPETIZER IS SIMPLE AND DELICIOUS

2 cups	cooked or canned chickpeas	500 mL
2 tbsp.	olive oil	30 mL
2 tsp.	salt	10 mL
1 tbsp.	tahini paste (sesame seed butter)	15 mL
2	garlic cloves, crushed	2
¼ cup	lemon juice	60 mL
¼ cup	chopped fresh parsley	60 mL
½	onion, chopped	½
1	celery stalk, chopped (optional)	1
	freshly ground pepper	
	fresh mint leaves (optional)	

- Place all ingredients, except pepper and mint, in a blender. Blend until a smooth paste is formed. Sprinkle with pepper and garnish with mint.
- Serve with pita bread, crackers or raw vegetables.

YIELD   *12 – 16 APPETIZER SERVINGS*

BLACK BEAN DIP

ADJUST "HEAT" LEVEL TO YOUR TASTE

19 oz.	can black turtle beans, drained	540 mL
2 tbsp.	hot salsa OR ketchup	30 mL
2	garlic cloves, crushed	2
1	lime, juice of	1
2 tbsp.	mayonnaise	30 mL
½ tsp.	EACH cumin & salt	2 mL
½ cup	finely chopped onion	125 mL
2 tbsp.	finely chopped jalapeño, or less, as you prefer	30 mL

BLACK BEAN DIP
(CONTINUED)

- In the bowl of a food processor, process all ingredients, except the onion and jalapeño, until a smooth paste is formed. Stir in onion and jalapeño.
- Refrigerate 2-3 hours to allow flavors to develop. Serve with tortilla chips, crackers or raw vegetables as dippers.

YIELD   *2 CUPS (500 ML)*

MEXICAN LAYERED DIP
GREAT FLAVOR AND EYE APPEAL, PLUS MAKE-AHEAD CONVENIENCE

14 oz.	can refried beans	398 mL
1 cup	guacamole, see page 44	250 mL
½ cup	sour cream	125 mL
⅓ cup	mayonnaise	75 mL
2 tsp.	taco seasoning	10 mL
3	green onions, chopped	3
2	tomatoes, diced	2
⅓ cup	sliced black olives	75 mL
3 oz.	grated Cheddar cheese	85 g
	tortilla chips	

- Spread beans in a 10" (25 cm) serving dish. Layer guacamole on top.
- Combine sour cream, mayonnaise and taco seasoning. Spread over guacamole.
- Continue to layer onions, tomatoes, olives and cheese.
- May be refrigerated up to 24 hours before serving. Serve with tortilla chips.

YIELD   *12 APPETIZER SERVINGS*

GUACAMOLE

MELLOW FLAVOR WITH A BITE!

1	avocado, peeled, mashed	1
1-2 tsp.	lemon juice	5-10 mL
2 tbsp.	finely chopped jalapeño OR hot pepper sauce to taste	30 mL
1 tsp.	salt	5 mL
1-2 tbsp.	grated onion	15-30 mL
1	Roma tomato, finely chopped	1

- In a small bowl, combine all ingredients.
- Cover tightly and refrigerate until ready to serve.
- Serve with tortilla chips, selected crackers or crudités.

YIELD   *1 CUP (250 ML)*

RED ONION SALSA

TART, WITH GREAT FRESH FLAVOR – ADJUST HEAT TO YOUR TASTE

½	red onion, finely chopped	½
2	Roma tomatoes, diced	2
2	green onions, chopped	2
2 tbsp.	chopped fresh basil or cilantro	30 mL
2 tbsp.	apple cider vinegar OR lime juice	30 mL
1 tbsp.	extra-virgin olive oil	15 mL
1 tsp.	soy sauce	5 mL
	hot pepper sauce to taste	
	tortilla chips	

- Combine red onion, tomatoes, green onion and basil.
- In a jar, combine vinegar, oil, soy sauce and pepper sauce. Shake well. Pour over onion mixture; toss lightly. Refrigerate for 2 hours.
- Serve with tortilla chips.

YIELD   *1½ CUPS (375 ML)*

MANGO TOMATO FRESH SALSA

ALSO USE PEACHES, PINEAPPLE OR PAPAYA – ADD HOT SAUCE TO TASTE

1	mango, finely diced	1
2	Roma tomatoes, diced	2
4	green onions, chopped	4
¼ cup	chopped fresh cilantro OR parsley	60 mL
1 tbsp.	lime juice	15 mL
1	garlic clove, crushed	1

- Place mango, tomatoes, onion and cilantro in a bowl.
- Combine lime juice and garlic. Toss with mango mixture.
- Serve with tortilla chips, also great with chicken or fish.

YIELD   2 – 3 CUPS (500 – 750 ML)

MANGO SALSA JELLY

A DELICIOUS GIFT FROM YOUR KITCHEN; ALSO SERVE WITH GRILLED CHICKEN

4	mangoes, diced	4
½	red pepper, finely chopped	½
½	onion, finely chopped	½
2-4	jalapeño peppers, finely chopped	2-4
2	garlic cloves, minced	2
¼ cup	chopped fresh cilantro OR parsley	60 mL
¼ cup	white vinegar	60 mL
2	limes, zest & juice of	2
7 cups	sugar	1.75 L
2 x 3 oz.	pouches of liquid fruit pectin	2 x 85 g

- Place all ingredients, except pectin, into a large saucepan. Over high heat, bring to a full rolling boil. Stir and boil for 1 minute; remove from heat.
- Immediately stir in pectin; stir for 5 minutes.
- Pour into hot sterilized jars, filling to ¼" (6 mm) from rim. While hot, seal with sterilized 2-piece lids. Let cool; label and store.
- Serve over cream cheese with assorted crackers.

YIELD   12, 8 OZ. (250 ML) JARS

Jazzabelle Spread

Jazzy flavor in an instant

8 oz.	jar pineapple, papaya & lime spread	250 mL
8 oz.	jar apple jelly	250 mL
2 tsp.	dry mustard	10 mL
½ cup	prepared horseradish	125 mL
1 tsp.	ground pepper	5 mL

- Combine all ingredients in a covered container. Refrigerate.
- Serve over cream cheese with assorted crackers.

YIELD   3 CUPS (750 ML)

Chilled Oysters with Lemon and Wine

Elegant – an old southern recipe with a subtle, addictive flavor

5 x 3 oz.	cans oysters (NOT smoked), drained	5 x 85 g
½ cup	olive oil	125 mL
¼ cup	fresh lemon juice	60 mL
2 tsp.	Worcestershire sauce	10 mL
2 tbsp.	chopped fresh parsley	30 mL
¼ cup	chopped onion	60 mL
¼ cup	white wine	60 mL
1 tsp.	EACH lemon pepper & salt	5 mL
½ tsp.	mustard seed OR pickling spice	2 mL
¼ tsp.	ground thyme	1 mL
¼ tsp.	EACH red pepper flakes & Tabasco	1 mL

- Place oysters in a medium bowl.
- Combine remaining ingredients and pour over oysters. Cover and refrigerate overnight or for several days. Toss occasionally to mix marinade.
- Serve chilled oysters with pumpernickel bread or melba toast.

YIELD   ABOUT 3 CUPS (750 ML)

SPICED NUTS
SUGAR-GLAZED AND SPICY

2 tbsp.	butter	30 mL
2 cups	nuts (unsalted cashews, peanuts, almonds, pecans OR walnuts)	500 mL
⅛ tsp.	EACH cinnamon, cloves & nutmeg	0.5 mL
2 tbsp.	sugar	30 mL

- In a heavy skillet, over medium-high heat, sauté nuts in butter for 2-3 minutes, or until lightly browned.
- In a medium bowl, combine spices and sugar. Toss with hot nuts.
- Transfer nuts to a parchment-lined cookie sheet; toast for 10-15 minutes at 300°F (150°C), or until nuts are dried and toasted.

VARIATION   *Ginger-Soy Nuts* – substitute 2 tbsp. (30 mL) soy sauce, ½ tsp. (2 mL) ground ginger and ½ tsp. (2 mL) garlic powder for the spice mixture.

YIELD   *2 CUPS (500 ML)*

HOT ONION TOASTIES
A QUICK HOT APPETIZER, ALSO SERVE WITH SOUPS

1	French baguette, sliced 1" (2.5 cm) thick	1
2 tbsp.	butter, softened	30 mL
1	onion, minced	1
3 tbsp.	mayonnaise	45 mL
¼ cup	grated Parmesan cheese	60 mL

- Butter baguette slices and top with onion. Spread mayonnaise on top. Sprinkle with Parmesan cheese.
- Place on a baking tray. Broil for 4-5 minutes. Serve hot.

YIELD   *16 – 20 APPETIZERS*

GRILLED CHEDDAR GARLIC LOAF

HEARTY AND HOT – VERY SATISFYING

1	loaf French bread	1
¼ cup	butter, softened	60 mL
1 cup	grated Cheddar cheese	250 mL
¼ cup	sour cream	60 mL
2	garlic cloves, minced	2
1 tbsp.	chopped fresh parsley	15 mL
1 tbsp.	chopped fresh dillweed	15 mL

- Slice bread in half lengthwise.
- Combine remaining ingredients. Spread on cut sides of bread.
- Grill for 5-7 minutes, until topping bubbles and bread is toasted.

YIELD   *10 – 12 SERVINGS*

SPINACH, SHRIMP AND CRAB IN A CANOE

IMPRESSIVE AND CONVENIENT – PREPARE IN THE MORNING; BAKE IN THE EVENING

10 oz.	pkg. frozen chopped spinach	283 g
1	medium onion, chopped	1
3½ oz.	can cocktail shrimp, drained	106 g
4½ oz.	can flaked crabmeat	120 g
6 oz.	Cheddar cheese, grated	170 g
10 oz.	can sliced mushrooms, drained	284 mL
1 cup	mayonnaise	250 mL
8 oz.	cream cheese, softened	250 g
1	garlic clove, crushed	1
2 tsp.	seasoned salt	10 mL
¼ tsp.	pepper	1 mL
2	French bread loaves	2

SPINACH, SHRIMP & CRAB IN A CANOE

(CONTINUED)

- Thaw spinach. Drain thoroughly, squeeze dry.
- Combine spinach with remaining ingredients, except bread.
- Cut a lengthwise slice from the top of each loaf. Hollow out loaves, leaving a ½" (1.3 cm) shell. Fill hollows with spinach dip. Replace lids.
- Wrap loaves in aluminum foil. Refrigerate until baking.
- Bake at 300°F (150°C) for 1½-2 hours, or until filling is heated through. Slice to serve.

YIELD   16 – 20 APPETIZER SERVINGS

SPINACH-STUFFED LOAF

ALWAYS POPULAR – WHITE CHEDDAR ADDS AN EXTRA BITE

1	large unsliced round loaf of sourdough OR French bread	1
8 oz.	light cream cheese, softened	250 g
⅔ cup	mayonnaise	150 mL
4 oz.	white extra-old Cheddar cheese, grated	120 g
10 oz.	pkg. frozen chopped spinach, thawed, cooked, drained	300 g
2 tbsp.	crisp, crumbled bacon	30 mL
1	garlic clove, crushed	1
¼ tsp.	freshly ground pepper	1 mL

- Cut a lengthwise slice off the top of the loaf of bread. Hollow out bread, leaving a 1" (2.5 cm) shell. Reserve removed bread.
- In a large bowl, combine all ingredients except bread.
- Fill bread with spinach mixture. Replace the top slice of bread.
- Double-wrap loaf in foil. If making ahead, refrigerate until baking.
- Bake at 325°F (160°C) for 1 hour, or until heated through.
- Serve with reserved bread and, if desired, vegetables for dipping.

YIELD   12 – 15 SERVINGS

MUSHROOMS WITH BRAZIL NUT STUFFING

MAKE AHEAD, REFRIGERATE AND BAKE WHEN READY TO SERVE – HOT AND TASTY

16	large mushrooms	16
2 tbsp.	butter	30 mL
1	small onion, chopped	1
½ cup	bread crumbs	125 mL
½ cup	chopped Brazil nuts	125 mL
½ tsp.	salt	2 mL
¼ tsp.	pepper	1 mL
2 tsp.	lemon juice	10 mL
2 tsp.	ketchup	10 mL
	crisp, crumbled bacon	
	cereal OR whipping cream	

- Clean mushrooms and remove stems. Finely chop stems.
- In a sauté pan, over medium heat, melt butter; sauté onions and stems for about 5 minutes. Add bread crumbs and chopped nuts; continue to cook for 2 minutes. Add salt, pepper, lemon juice and ketchup.
- Stuff mushrooms caps with bread mixture. Arrange stuffed mushrooms in a shallow, ovenproof dish. Garnish with bacon. Drizzle cream over and around mushroom caps.
- Bake at 375°F (200°C) for 15 minutes, or until lightly browned.

VARIATIONS   For **Shrimp-** or **Crab-Stuffed Mushrooms**, substitute ½ cup (125 mL) of chopped cooked shrimp or crab for Brazil nuts. Use 1 tbsp. (15 mL) mayonnaise instead of ketchup.

For **Sausage-Stuffed Mushrooms**, substitute 6 oz. (170 g) sautéed, chopped pork sausage for Brazil nuts. Add 1 minced garlic clove. Omit ketchup and cream.

YIELD   *16 APPETIZERS*

STUFFED GRAPE LEAVES (DOLMADES)

LIVELY LEMON SPARKS THIS GREEK AND MIDDLE EASTERN APPETIZER OR SIDE DISH

½ cup	pine nuts	125 mL
1	medium onion, chopped	1
1 tsp.	salt	5 mL
1 tbsp.	olive oil	15 mL
1 cup	orzo pasta	250 mL
1 tbsp.	fresh lemon juice	15 mL
½ cup	EACH chopped fresh parsley & dillweed	125 mL
¼ tsp.	pepper	1 mL
8 oz.	feta cheese, crumbled	250 g
1 tsp.	crushed dried basil	5 mL
16 oz.	jar bottled grape leaves in brine	500 mL
½ cup	olive oil	125 mL
2 tbsp.	fresh lemon juice	30 mL
½ cup	boiling water	125 mL
	fresh lemon juice	

- Place pine nuts on an ungreased cookie sheet. Toast at 350°F (180°C) for 5 minutes. Chop coarsely; set aside.
- In a skillet, sweat onion with salt over very low heat for 5 minutes, or until onion is wilted. Increase heat to medium, add 1 tbsp. (15 mL) oil, orzo and lemon juice. Sauté for 2 minutes. Add parsley, dill and pepper. Sauté for 2 minutes. Remove from heat. Add pine nuts, feta and basil.
- Drain brine from grape leaves. Unroll leaves; rinse in cold water; drain.
- Lay leaves flat, underside up, on a work surface. Trim thick stem portions; cut large leaves in half.
- Place 1 tsp. (5 mL) of orzo mixture on the base of each leaf. Roll tightly, folding sides in, to enclose filling.
- Place rolls tightly against others in an ovenproof dish.
- Combine ½ cup (125 mL) olive oil, lemon juice and boiling water. Pour over stuffed leaves. Bake at 350°F (180°C) for 30 to 40 minutes.
- Serve warm or cold with additional lemon juice sprinkled over.

YIELD   ***ABOUT 60 DOLMADES***

GREEN ONION CAKES

DELICIOUS SAVORY APPETIZER PANCAKES

2 cups	all-purpose flour	500 mL
½ tsp.	sugar	2 mL
⅔ cup	boiling water	150 mL
⅓ cup	cold water	75 mL
2 tsp.	sesame oil	10 mL
1½ tsp.	salt	7 mL
½ tsp.	pepper (optional)	2 mL
½ cup	minced green onions	125 mL
¾ cup	vegetable oil for frying	175 mL

- In a medium bowl, combine flour and sugar. Pour in boiling water, stirring until all water is absorbed. Stir in just enough cold water to form a soft, not sticky dough that pulls away from the bowl.
- Knead dough on a floured surface until smooth and elastic, about 5 minutes. Cover with a damp towel and let rest for 45-60 minutes.
- Knead dough again on a floured surface for 4-5 minutes, until smooth and elastic. Divide dough into 4 portions. Work with 1 at a time, keeping others covered.
- Roll 1 dough portion into a 7" (18 cm) circle. Brush with sesame oil and sprinkle with ¼ of the salt and green onions. Roll up circle into a long cylinder, coiling into a flat cake and pinching the end to seal it. Repeat for other portions. Cover cakes with a damp towel and let rest for 20 minutes.
- On a floured surface, roll cakes into 7" (18 cm) circles.
- Heat oil to 365°F (185°C) in a deep skillet or wok. Fry 1 cake at a time, about 2 minutes, until golden. Turn cake over and fry again until slightly browned. Drain on paper towels. Repeat with remaining cakes.
- Sprinkle cakes with salt, cut into wedges and serve warm with Chili Lime Sauce or Szechuan Sauce, page 118, or a garlic chili sauce for dipping.

YIELD   4 GREEN ONION CAKES

Soups & Stews

Chilled and refreshing or hearty and
comforting, these soups are easy to
prepare and satisfying year round. The
stews are substantial – full-bodied meals
in a bowl to serve after a day at work or a
day of outdoor fun. Serve soups or stews
with crusty breads and a tossed salad for
family lunches or dinners or for
casual entertaining.

ICY PEACH & BLUEBERRY SOUP

BEAUTIFUL PRESENTATION – ALSO DELICIOUS WITH MANGOES OR NECTARINES

1 cup	water	250 mL
¼ tsp.	EACH cinnamon, nutmeg & cloves	1 mL
1-2 tbsp.	sugar	15-30 mL
1 tbsp.	cornstarch	15 mL
¼ cup	water	60 mL
2 lbs.	fresh peaches peeled, pitted OR 28 oz. (796 mL) can sliced peaches	1 kg
1 cup	white wine	250 mL
2 cups	thinly sliced peeled peaches	500 mL
1 cup	sour cream OR plain yogurt for garnish	250 mL
1 cup	blueberries for garnish	250 mL

- In a small saucepan, bring 1 cup (250 mL) water, any juices from sliced or canned peaches, spices and sugar to a boil. Dissolve cornstarch in ¼ cup (60 mL) water; stir into simmering liquid until thickened.
- Purée 2 lbs. (1 kg) of peaches in a blender or food processor.
- Pour water mixture into a large non-metal bowl. Stir in wine, peach purée and sliced peaches. Refrigerate, covered, for several hours.
- Garnish each serving with sour cream and blueberries.

YIELD   6 – 8 SERVINGS

COLD CHERRY SOUP

ADD A SPLASH OF KIRSCH IF YOU WISH

2 cups	warm water	500 mL
½ cup	sugar	125 mL
2 tbsp.	lemon juice	30 mL
2 lbs.	fresh cherries, stemmed, pitted, halved	1 kg
1 cup	cherry-flavored yogurt	250 mL

- In a large bowl, dissolve sugar in water. Add lemon juice.
- Reserve a few cherries for garnish. In a food processor, purée remaining cherries with some sugar syrup. Stir purée and yogurt into syrup.
- Chill soup. Serve garnished with cherry halves and additional yogurt.

YIELD   6 CUPS (1.5 L)

SPICY GAZPACHO

THIS CRUNCHY CHILLED SOUP IS WONDERFULLY REFRESHING
ON A HOT SUMMER DAY

2 lbs.	fresh tomatoes, peeled OR 28 oz. (796 mL) can diced tomatoes	1 kg
1	large green or red pepper, seeded, finely chopped	1
2	garlic cloves, finely chopped	2
¾ cup	fresh mixed herbs, chopped (chives, parsley, basil, chervil, tarragon)	175 mL
1	large Spanish onion, peeled, finely chopped	1
1	large cucumber, peeled, finely chopped	1
½ cup	vegetable OR olive oil	125 mL
⅓ cup	lemon juice	75 mL
4 cups	tomato juice	1 L
2 tbsp.	red wine vinegar	30 mL
2 tsp.	salt	10 mL
½ tsp.	paprika	2 mL
½ tsp.	freshly ground black pepper	2 mL
1 tsp.	Worcestershire sauce, or more, to taste	5 mL
½ tsp.	Tabasco sauce, or more, to taste	2 mL
	Oil & Garlic Croûtons for garnish, see page 58	
	chopped fresh herbs for garnish	

- Purée tomatoes in a blender; pour purée into a 4-quart (4 L) glass or plastic container. Add chopped pepper, garlic, herbs, onion and cucumber. Stir well. Stir in oil, lemon and tomato juices, vinegar, salt, paprika, pepper, Worcestershire and Tabasco. Cover and chill at least 4 hours, or overnight, before serving.
- Garnish each serving with Oil & Garlic Croûtons and chopped fresh herbs. For a summer party you might want to add 1 oz. (30 mL) of vodka to each serving.
- Refrigerated, this soup will remain fresh and crunchy for several days.

YIELD   *10 – 12 SERVINGS*

COLD TOMATO & ORANGE SOUP

A REAL SURPRISE – LIGHT, TANGY AND VERY EASY TO MAKE

2 cups	EACH tomato & orange juice	500 mL
½ cup	dry white wine	125 mL
1	lemon, juice of	1
1 tsp.	sugar	5 mL
1½ tsp.	salt	7 mL
¼ tsp.	cayenne pepper	1 mL
	chopped parsley for garnish	

- In a large bowl or pitcher, combine all ingredients, except parsley. Chill.
- Serve very cold, sprinkled with chopped parsley.

YIELD   *6 – 8 SERVINGS*

FRESH ASPARAGUS SOUP

MELLOW, UNBEATABLE FLAVOR

2 tbsp.	vegetable oil	30 mL
1	medium onion, chopped	1
2	celery stalks, chopped	2
4 cups	chicken stock	1 L
12 oz.	fresh asparagus spears	340 g
1	large potato, peeled, chopped	1
½ tsp.	salt	2 mL
¼ tsp.	EACH pepper and nutmeg	1 mL
1½ cups	milk	375 mL

- In a large saucepan, heat oil; sauté onion and celery until tender. Add chicken stock and bring to a boil.
- Cut tips off asparagus spears; add to stock and cook until tender crisp, about 2 minutes. Remove tips; run under cold water; set aside.
- Chop remaining asparagus. Add to stock with potato, salt, pepper and nutmeg. Reduce heat; cover and cook until potato is tender.
- Purée soup in a blender or use a hand processor.
- Add milk and reserved tips to purée. Heat until hot but not boiling.

YIELD   *6 SERVINGS*

Avgolemono

A classic Greek egg and lemon soup – tart and terrific

8 cups	chicken stock	2 L
1 cup	orzo OR long-grain rice	250 mL
4	eggs, separated	4
3	lemons, juice of, adjust to taste	3
	salt & freshly ground pepper to taste	
	minced parsley for garnish	
	lemon slices for garnish	

- In a large saucepan, bring stock to a boil. Add orzo or rice and cook until tender, about 15 minutes.
- In a medium bowl, beat egg whites until soft peaks form. Beat in yolks and lemon juice until thoroughly blended.
- Beat in 2 cups (500 mL) stock, pouring in slowly and beating continuously, to temper eggs.
- Whisk eggs into soup. Serve hot, garnished with parsley and lemon slices.
- To reheat soup, do not boil; heat slowly or soup may curdle.

VARIATIONS   Add 1-2 cups (250-500 mL) shredded cooked chicken or turkey. For a much less authentic, but delicious, variation stir in 3-4 cups (750 mL-1 L) shredded fresh spinach leaves just before whisking in the eggs.

YIELD   **6 – 8 SERVINGS**

Orzo is a small rice-shaped pasta used in soups and side dishes. The name means barley kernels in Italian. For a side dish, toss hot cooked orzo with olive oil, crushed garlic, chopped fresh basil, oregano and chives, Parmesan cheese, salt and pepper.

CREAM OF BROCCOLI SOUP

FOR MAXIMUM FLAVOR, SPRINKLE WITH CRUMBLED CHEDDAR OR BLUE CHEESE

2 cups	chopped broccoli, florets & stems	500 mL
1 tbsp.	olive oil	15 mL
2	celery stalks, chopped	2
1	medium onion, chopped	1
4 cups	chicken or vegetable stock	1 L
2 tbsp.	butter	30 mL
2 tbsp.	flour	30 mL
1 cup	half 'n' half (cereal) cream	250 mL
½ tsp.	freshly ground pepper	2 mL
	salt to taste	

- In a medium soup pot, heat oil over medium heat, sauté broccoli stem pieces, onion and celery until tender. Add stock and cook for 8-10 minutes. Add broccoli florets.
- In a small saucepan over low heat, melt butter. Add flour and cream. Cook and stir until thickened and bubbly. Stir into soup until thoroughly heated. Season to taste.

YIELD   **4 SERVINGS**

BAKED CROÛTONS

ADD CRUNCH TO SOUPS AND SALADS

- Brush slices of crusty bread with olive oil. Sprinkle with dried thyme. Cut into ½" (1.3 cm) cubes. Place on a baking sheet and bake at 350°F (180°C), tossing frequently, for 15 minutes, or until crisp. Add to soups or salads.

VARIATIONS   For **Oil & Garlic Croûtons**, omit thyme and generously sprinkle cubed bread with garlic powder.
For **Parmesan Garlic Croûtons**, sprinkle Parmesan cheese over Oil & Garlic Croûtons. Bake as above for both variations.

CORN POTATO CHOWDER

THICK AND RICH — AN OUTSTANDING MEAL IN A BOWL

2 tbsp.	vegetable oil	30 mL
1	medium onion, chopped	1
2	celery stalks, chopped	2
¼ lb.	sausage, ham OR back bacon, diced	100 g
3 cups	chicken stock	750 mL
3	potatoes, peeled, diced	3
2	cobs of corn OR 12 oz. (341 mL) can of kernel corn	2
¼ tsp.	salt	1 mL
¼ tsp.	pepper	1 mL
½ tsp.	Worcestershire sauce	2 mL
¼ tsp.	hot pepper sauce (optional)	1 mL
1 cup	half 'n' half (cereal) cream	250 mL

- In a large, heavy-bottomed pot, heat oil and sauté onion and celery until tender. Add sausage; sauté a few more minutes.
- Add stock and bring to a boil. Add diced potatoes.
- Remove corn kernels from the cob. Add corn, salt, pepper and Worcestershire sauce to soup. Reduce heat; boil gently until corn kernels are tender and potatoes no longer hold their shape. Stir well so potatoes break apart and thicken the soup.
- Add cream; heat thoroughly but do NOT boil.

VARIATION   For **Salmon Chowder**, omit sausage. Corn is optional; use fish stock instead of chicken stock. Add 12 oz. (340 g) salmon fillet to soup after potatoes have cooked for 10 minutes. Cook salmon for about 10 minutes, or until it flakes readily. Flake salmon and add cream as above. Garnish with dill sprigs.

YIELD   **6 SERVINGS**

TORTELLINI SPINACH SOUP

GARLIC AND HERBS ENHANCE THE FRESH FLAVOR OF SPINACH

1 tbsp.	olive oil	15 mL
2	carrots, grated	2
1	medium onion, chopped	1
2	garlic cloves, minced	2
8 cups	chicken stock	2 L
12 oz.	pkg. fresh tortellini	340 g
6 oz.	pkg. fresh baby spinach	170 g
1 tsp.	crushed sweet basil	5 mL
½ tsp.	crushed oregano leaves	2 mL
	salt & pepper to taste	
	shredded mozzarella cheese (optional)	

- In a Dutch oven, heat oil. Sauté carrots, onion and garlic until tender. Add the stock; bring to a boil.
- Add tortellini; boil gently for 4 to 5 minutes. Add spinach and seasonings; simmer 2 to 3 minutes, or until spinach is tender.
- Serve hot, sprinkled with shredded mozzarella cheese if desired.

YIELD   *6 SERVINGS*

Spinach was brought to North America from Spain. In Italy, spinach is so popular that recipes featuring it are often called "à la Florentine". Rich in iron, vitamins A and C, its slightly bitter flavor is enhanced by both tart and rich flavors – cheeses, butter, lemon, garlic, eggs, oysters, mushrooms and bacon. Spinach stars in soups, salads, pasta and seafood dishes.

ITALIAN PASTA & WHITE BEAN SOUP (PASTA E FAGIOLI)

A VERSATILE HEARTY WINTER SOUP THAT IS A MEAL IN ITSELF!

1 cup	dried cannelloni OR white kidney beans	250 mL
	water	
1 tbsp.	vegetable oil	15 mL
1 lb.	ground beef	450 g
1	onion, chopped	1
1	carrot, chopped	1
2	celery stalks, chopped	2
4	plum tomatoes, peeled, seeded, chopped	4
4 cups	beef stock	1 L
2 tsp.	dried oregano	10 mL
1 tsp.	EACH pepper & salt	5 mL
1 tbsp.	chopped fresh parsley	15 mL
½-1 tsp.	hot pepper sauce	2-5 mL
½ cup	small dry pasta	125 mL
	additional beef stock OR tomato juice	
	freshly grated Parmesan cheese	

- Soak beans overnight in water to cover; drain. In a stockpot, cook beans in water to cover until almost tender, about 1 hour. Drain; return beans to pot.
- In a skillet, heat oil; sauté beef until browned. Add onion, carrot, celery and tomatoes; simmer for 10 minutes, or until vegetables are soft.
- To beans in stockpot, add beef and sautéed vegetables, beef stock and seasonings. Cook over low heat for 30 minutes.
- Add pasta and cook for about 10 minutes, or until pasta is still slightly firm. Add additional stock or juice if soup is too thick.
- To serve, adjust seasonings; sprinkle each serving with Parmesan cheese.

YIELD   8 – 10 SERVINGS

See photograph on page 67.

HERBED SALMON BISQUE

AROMATIC ROSEMARY IS WONDERFUL WITH SALMON

2 tbsp.	vegetable oil	30 mL
1	onion, chopped	1
½	red OR green pepper, chopped	½
2	celery stalks, chopped	2
2	carrots, chopped	2
2	potatoes, peeled, diced	2
2 cups	fish stock OR water	500 mL
2 cups	milk	500 mL
14 oz.	can creamed corn	398 mL
8 oz.	cooked salmon, flaked	250 g
½ tsp.	salt	2 mL
¼ tsp.	pepper	1 mL
2 tsp.	dried parsley	10 mL
1 tsp.	dried rosemary	5 mL

- In a Dutch oven, heat oil; sauté onion, pepper, celery, carrots and potatoes until slightly tender.
- Add stock and bring to a boil. Reduce heat and simmer for 15 minutes.
- Stir in the milk, corn, salmon, salt and pepper. Continue to simmer until vegetables are tender.
- Add parsley and rosemary; simmer for 2 minutes.

VARIATION   Substitute other fish or seafood for the salmon.

YIELD   *6 – 8 SERVINGS*

Salmon, long prized for its succulent flavor, rich color and silky texture, is now highly recommended as an excellent source of Omega-3 fatty acids. It is also a good source of protein, the B vitamins and vitamin A.

Hot Shrimp Soup with Peppers

PEPPERS ADD LIVELY COLOR AND FRESH ZESTY FLAVOR

2 tbsp.	olive oil	30 mL
1	large onion, chopped	1
4	garlic cloves, minced	4
1	red pepper, chopped	1
1	green pepper, chopped	1
1	yellow pepper, chopped	1
1	jalapeño pepper, finely chopped	1
28 oz.	can Italian-style peeled tomatoes, chopped	796 mL
3 cups	chicken stock	750 mL
19 oz.	can black beans, drained, rinsed	540 mL
½ tsp.	hot pepper sauce (optional)	2 mL
8 oz.	bite-sized, cooked, fresh shrimp	250 g
2 tbsp.	fresh lime juice	30 mL
¼ tsp.	ground coriander OR 1 tsp. (5 mL) chopped fresh cilantro	1 mL
	grated Cheddar cheese for garnish	
	chopped green onions for garnish	

- In a large, heavy-bottomed saucepan, heat oil over medium heat.
- Add onion, garlic and peppers. Cook for 5 minutes.
- Add tomatoes, stock, beans and pepper sauce. Bring to a boil; reduce heat and simmer for 20 minutes.
- Add shrimp, lime juice and coriander. Simmer for 2-3 minutes.
- Garnish individual servings with cheese and onions.

YIELD   *12 SERVINGS*

CHICKEN KALE SOUP

NUTRITIOUS KALE IS POPULAR IN NORTHERN EUROPEAN CUISINE

1 tbsp.	olive oil	15 mL
½ tsp.	crushed red pepper flakes	2 mL
1	bay leaf, crushed	1
½	medium onion, chopped	½
2	garlic cloves, minced	2
1	chicken breast, cubed	1
2	medium potatoes, peeled, cubed	2
6 cups	chicken stock	1.5 L
6-8 cups	lightly packed, shredded kale	1.5-2 L
2-3 tbsp.	lemon juice OR vinegar	30-45 mL
	salt & pepper to taste	

- In a heavy stockpot, heat oil. Add pepper flakes, bay leaf, onion, garlic and chicken. Sauté until onion is translucent and chicken is browned.
- Add potatoes and stock. Bring to a boil; turn down heat and cook until potatoes are tender. Add kale, lemon juice, salt and pepper. Cook briefly, just until kale is tender. Adjust seasonings.

VARIATION   Substitute sorrel, spinach, swiss chard, or beet leaves for the kale.

YIELD   *6 SERVINGS*

BEEF STOCK

YOUR SOUP IS ONLY AS GOOD AS YOUR STOCK!

1 tbsp.	EACH butter & olive oil	15 mL
3-4 lbs.	meaty beef soup bones	1.5-2 kg
2	carrots, chopped	2
1	medium onion, chopped	1
4 cups	water	1 L
1 cup	dry red wine	250 mL
2	bay leaves	2
2	celery stalks with leaves, chopped	2
10	whole peppercorns	10

BEEF STOCK

(CONTINUED)

- In a Dutch oven, heat butter and oil and brown meat, carrots and onion.
- Add remaining ingredients; cover. Bring to a boil. Reduce heat and cook at a slow boil until meat is tender, 1½ to 2 hours.
- Strain mixture, reserving meat and stock separately. Cool stock.
- Remove congealed fat from surface of cooled stock.
- Remove meat from bones and chop into bite-sized pieces.
- Freeze any unused stock and meat in separate containers.

YIELD   *4 CUPS (1 L) STOCK*

SOUTH-OF-THE-BORDER TURKEY SOUP

A TASTY, SPICY MEAL IN A BOWL

1 tbsp.	EACH vegetable oil & butter	15 mL
1	onion, chopped	1
1¼ lbs.	ground turkey OR chicken	575 g
1	jalapeño pepper, seeded, finely chopped	1
½	EACH green & red pepper, chopped	½
1 tbsp.	taco seasoning, see page 142	15 mL
2	plum tomatoes, chopped	2
1½ cups	corn kernels	375 mL
6 cups	chicken stock	1.5 L
	freshly grated pepper & salt to taste	
	sour cream, fresh parsley, grated Monterey Jack cheese, crushed corn tortilla chips for garnish	

- In a large heavy stockpot, heat oil and butter over medium heat. Add onion; cook until translucent. Add turkey; sauté until no longer pink.
- Add peppers and taco seasoning; sauté until peppers are tender.
- Add tomatoes, corn, chicken stock and pepper. Bring to a boil; reduce heat. Simmer for 45-60 minutes. Add salt to taste.
- Serve hot and garnish individual servings.

YIELD   *8 SERVINGS*

Turkey Barley Soup

AN UPDATED SCOTCH BROTH – A GREAT WINTER SOUP

1 tbsp.	EACH butter & olive oil	15 mL
1	celery stalk, chopped	1
1	medium onion, chopped	1
6 cups	turkey stock	1.5 L
½ cup	pearl barley	125 mL
1	carrot, diced	1
1	potato, peeled, cubed	1
1½ cups	cooked diced turkey	375 mL
½ tsp.	salt	2 mL
¼ tsp.	pepper	1 mL
2	bay leaves	2
½ cup	frozen peas	125 mL
1-2 cups	milk	250-500 mL

- In a heavy stockpot, heat butter and oil; sauté celery and onion until tender.
- Add stock, barley, carrot, potato, turkey, salt, pepper and bay leaves. Simmer gently until barley is tender, about 45 minutes.
- Add frozen peas; simmer for 5 minutes.
- Just prior to serving, add milk to obtain desired consistency. Remove bay leaves.

YIELD   6 SERVINGS

 Featuring a nutty roasted flavor, barley has been used since 7,000 B.C. in soups, breads and cereals. It is also used to make beer and Scotch whisky. Pearl barley has the husk, bran and germ removed. It cooks in about 45 minutes and keeps for about 6 months in an airtight container. Pot (Scotch) barley is soaked overnight, drained, then cooked for 1-1½ hours in 4-5 times the volume of liquid.

SOUP & SALAD

Italian Pasta & White Bean Soup, page 61
Wilted Spinach Salad, page 82
Focaccia, page 19

HEARTY HUNTER'S SOUP

TRY THIS COUNTRY SOUP WITH ELK, VENISON OR CARIBOU

2 tbsp.	vegetable oil	30 mL
1 lb.	ground moose meat OR ground beef	500 g
1	medium onion, chopped	1
2	celery stalks, chopped	2
2	garlic cloves, minced	2
4 cups	beef stock	1 L
28 oz.	can tomatoes	796 mL
14 oz.	can tomato sauce	398 mL
4	carrots, chopped	4
4	potatoes, cubed	4
2	bay leaves	2
1 tsp.	EACH dried thyme, oregano & basil	5 mL
1 tsp.	salt	5 mL
½ tsp.	pepper	2 mL

- In a Dutch oven, over medium heat, heat oil and brown meat. Add onion, celery and garlic; continue to sauté until onion is translucent.
- Add remaining ingredients. Bring to a boil. Cover; reduce heat and cook slowly until vegetables are tender, about 30 minutes.
- If desired, extra stock may be added to obtain the desired consistency.

VARIATION Barley, rice or pasta may be added, with the vegetables, to extend or vary the soup.

YIELD **8 SERVINGS**

BEEF GOULASH SOUP

HUNGARIAN PAPRIKA ADDS SPICY SWEETNESS

2 cups	beef stock	500 mL
1 cup	water	250 mL
2 cups	chopped cooked beef	500 mL
2	potatoes, peeled, cubed	2
1	medium onion, chopped	1
2	garlic cloves, minced	2
1 tsp.	dried thyme	5 mL
8 oz.	can tomato sauce	250 mL
2 tbsp.	red wine vinegar	30 mL
2 tsp.	Worcestershire sauce	10 mL
¼ cup	flour	60 mL
2 tbsp.	Hungarian paprika	30 mL
½ cup	water	125 mL
1 cup	frozen peas	250 mL
	salt & pepper to taste	

- In a large saucepan, combine stock, 1 cup (250 mL) water, beef, potatoes, onion, garlic, thyme, tomato sauce, vinegar and Worcestershire sauce. Bring to a gentle boil and cook until vegetables are tender.
- In a small bowl, combine flour, Hungarian paprika and water.
- Add peas to goulash. Bring to a quick boil. Add the flour mixture, stirring until thickened and bubbly. Cook for an additional 2 minutes.
- Season with salt and pepper.

VARIATION   For **Hungarian Goulash**, use half of the stock and omit the water. Serve over noodles with a dollop of sour cream.

YIELD   **4 – 6 SERVINGS**

 Paprikas, made of ground dried ripe sweet peppers, vary in color and flavor, from orange to dark red, from mild to fiery. Hungarian paprika, an essential part of Hungarian cuisine, is considered to be the best. It is available in both hot and mild versions.

LENTIL SAUSAGE POTAGE

THICK AND GARLICKY – A FULL-BODIED SOUP –
PERFECT AFTER A DAY OF SKIING OR SNOWMOBILING

1 tbsp.	vegetable oil	15 mL
4 slices	smoked maple ham OR bacon, chopped	4 slices
1	onion, chopped	1
½	green pepper, chopped	½
2	garlic cloves, crushed	2
1	carrot, chopped	1
1	celery stalk, chopped	1
2 qts.	beef stock	2 L
1 cup	lentils, rinsed in cold water	250 mL
2	bay leaves	2
¼ tsp.	ground thyme	1 mL
1 cup	instant potato flakes	250 mL
1 tbsp.	apple cider vinegar	15 mL
	salt & pepper to taste	
½	ring of garlic or ham sausage, coarsely chopped	½

- In a Dutch oven, heat oil. Sauté ham, onion, green pepper, garlic, carrot and celery, until vegetables are just tender.
- Add stock, lentils, bay leaves and thyme. Bring soup to a boil.
- Reduce heat; simmer for 30 minutes, or until lentils are tender. Remove bay leaves.
- Add remaining ingredients; cook an additional few minutes until soup is thickened and sausage is thoroughly heated.

NOTE   Potato flakes are used to thicken the soup. If you prefer, shake 2-3 tbsp. (30-45 mL) of flour in ½ cup (125 mL) of water until smooth. Stir into soup to thicken.

YIELD   *6 – 8 SERVINGS*

Pork Ragoût with Sweet Potatoes and Apricots

DOUBLES, TRIPLES AND FREEZES WELL – TENDER, SAVORY AND SWEET

2 tbsp.	Dijon mustard	30 mL
¾ lb.	pork loin boneless chops, trimmed of fat, cubed	340 g
2 tbsp.	brown sugar	30 mL
2 tbsp.	all-purpose flour	30 mL
½ tsp.	salt	2 mL
¼ tsp.	freshly ground pepper	1 mL
2 tbsp.	vegetable oil	30 mL
½	onion, chopped	½
1	garlic clove, crushed	1
½ cup	chicken stock	125 mL
2	sweet potatoes, peeled, cubed	2
½ cup	halved, dried apricots	125 mL

- Place mustard and cubed pork into a plastic bag; shake to coat pork. Combine sugar, flour, salt and pepper. Add to plastic bag and dredge mustard-covered pork in flour mixture.
- In a Dutch oven, heat oil over medium heat. Brown pork in oil. Add onion and garlic and continue to cook until onion is softened. Stir in chicken stock, scraping up browned bits on bottom of pan. Add sweet potatoes and apricot halves. Combine well.
- Reduce heat to low; cover. Cook, stirring occasionally, for 45 minutes, or until tender.
- Serve over a bed of rice or noodles with a tossed salad or vegetable.

VARIATIONS   Substitute apple cider or juice, or even half juice and half beer, for the chicken stock. For a Mediterranean flavor, add ¼ tsp. (1 mL) each ground coriander and cinnamon, plus ¼ cup (60 mL) chopped pitted prunes.

YIELD   *6 SERVINGS*

"GONE-ALL-DAY" STEW

COME HOME TO THE WELCOMING AROMA OF THIS SAVORY STEW

2 lbs.	stewing beef, cubed	1 kg
2 tbsp.	vegetable oil	30 mL
1	onion, chopped	1
2	garlic cloves, minced	2
1	celery stalk, chopped	1
1 cup	crushed tomatoes OR 5½ oz. (156 mL) tomato paste	250 mL
1¼ cups	water	300 mL
¼ cup	flour	60 mL
3	carrots, sliced	3
3	white onions, quartered	3
4	potatoes, quartered	4
12	mushrooms, sliced	12
2 tsp.	dried beef bouillon	10 mL
1 tsp.	dried oregano flakes	5 mL
1 tsp.	ground thyme	5 mL
1 tsp.	dried rosemary leaves	5 mL
1 tsp.	salt	5 mL
½ tsp.	pepper	2 mL

- In a skillet, heat oil and brown meat. Add onion, garlic and celery; cook until vegetables are tender. Spoon into a slow cooker.
- Combine tomatoes, water and flour until smooth. Add to slow cooker; mix well.
- Stir in remaining ingredients. Cook for 4-6 hours, or until vegetables are thoroughly cooked.

YIELD   *8 SERVINGS*

HOT TORNADO STEW

GUTSY FLAVOR – BEER, SALSA AND PEPPERS

1 lb.	stewing beef, in ½" (1 cm) cubes	500 g
2 tbsp.	vegetable oil	30 mL
1	medium onion, chopped	1
1	celery stalk, chopped	1
2	garlic cloves, minced	2
5½ oz.	can tomato paste	156 mL
12 oz.	can vegetable cocktail juice	340 mL
2	canned roasted red peppers, chopped	2
12⅔ oz.	can beer	355 mL
¼ cup	salsa	60 mL
½ tsp.	cayenne pepper	2 mL
½ tsp.	salt	2 mL
1 tsp.	chili powder	5 mL
¼ tsp.	celery seed	1 mL
¼ tsp.	hot pepper sauce (optional)	1 mL
4	potatoes, peeled, cubed	4

- In a large heavy-bottomed pan, over medium heat, heat oil and brown meat. Add onion, celery and garlic; cook for 3 minutes.
- Add remaining ingredients. Lower heat; simmer, stirring occasionally, for 2 hours, or until meat and potatoes are tender.

YIELD   4 – 5 SERVINGS

Sweet 'n' Sour Stew

TANGY AND SWEET – SATISFYING AND FLAVORFUL

2 tbsp.	flour	30 mL
½ tsp.	salt	2 mL
1½ lbs.	round steak, cubed	675 g
2 tbsp.	vegetable oil	30 mL
1½ cups	beef stock	375 mL
5½ oz.	can tomato paste	156 mL
2 tbsp.	brown sugar	30 mL
¼ cup	white vinegar	60 mL
1 tbsp.	Worcestershire sauce	15 mL
1	onion, chopped	1
3	carrots, chopped	3
3	potatoes, cubed	3
½	rutabaga OR turnip, diced	½
¼ tsp.	black pepper	1 mL

- In a plastic bag, combine flour and salt. Add beef and shake to coat.
- In a Dutch oven, heat oil and brown meat. Reduce heat to low.
- Add stock, tomato paste, sugar, vinegar, Worcestershire sauce and onion. Simmer for 45 minutes.
- Add remaining vegetables and pepper. Continue to cook for 45 minutes, or until meat and vegetables are tender.

YIELD   6 SERVINGS

Turnip or rutabaga? Sometimes these terms are used interchangeably, but they are two distinct cruciferous vegetables. The turnip has a white skin with a purple-hued top. The flesh is white. The rutabaga has pale yellow skin and flesh. Originally from Sweden, it is also called a Swedish turnip or Swede. Smaller, heavy-for-their-size turnips and rutabagas are the best choice. They may be used interchangeably in recipes.

IRISH LAMB STEW

TENDER LAMB IN A RICH BROTH – A CLASSIC WITH DUMPLINGS

1 tbsp.	vegetable oil	15 mL
1½ lbs.	lamb, cut into 1" (2.5 cm) cubes	680 g
2	onions, chopped	2
4	potatoes, peeled, cubed	4
4 cups	beef stock	1 L
½ tsp.	salt	2 mL
¼ tsp.	EACH pepper, celery seed, dried marjoram, dried thyme	1 mL
10 oz.	package frozen peas	285 g
¼ cup	flour	60 mL
½ cup	cold water	125 mL

- In a Dutch oven, heat oil and brown meat. Add onions, potatoes, stock, spices and herbs. Cook on low for 1 hour, or until vegetables are tender.
- Shake flour with water until smooth. Stir into stew with the peas.
- Increase heat; stir and cook until gravy is thickened.
- Add dumplings if desired, see recipe below.

YIELD   4 – 6 SERVINGS

DUMPLINGS

FOR HERBED DUMPLINGS, ADD CHOPPED PARSLEY, THYME OR CHIVES

1 cup	all-purpose flour	250 mL
1½ tsp.	baking powder	7 mL
½ tsp.	salt	2 mL
½ cup	buttermilk	125 mL

- In a medium bowl, combine flour, baking powder and salt.
- Gradually, stir in buttermilk until a light, soft dough is formed.
- Carefully drop small spoonfuls of dough into cooked stew. Cover and simmer for an additional 15 minutes.

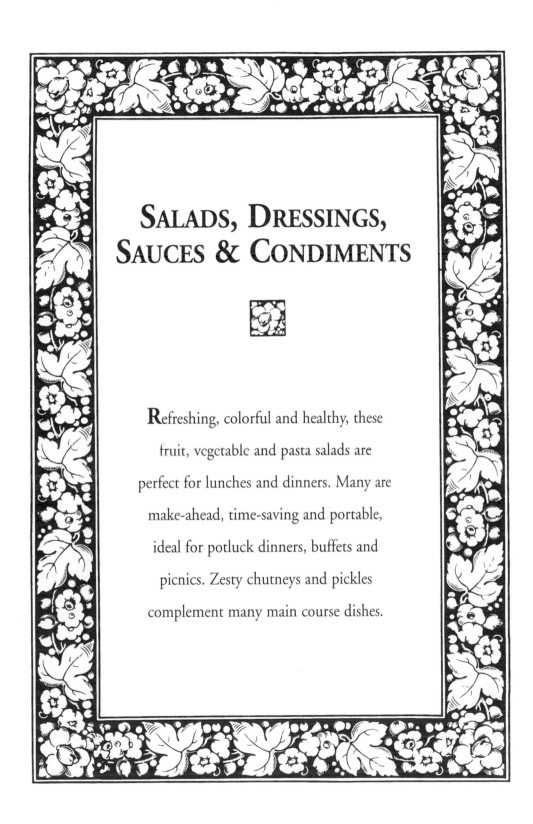

SALADS, DRESSINGS, SAUCES & CONDIMENTS

Refreshing, colorful and healthy, these
fruit, vegetable and pasta salads are
perfect for lunches and dinners. Many are
make-ahead, time-saving and portable,
ideal for potluck dinners, buffets and
picnics. Zesty chutneys and pickles
complement many main course dishes.

HORSERADISH MOLDED SALAD

DELICIOUS WITH ROAST BEEF OR BARBECUED STEAK

3 oz.	pkg. lemon gelatin	85 g
1 cup	boiling water	250 mL
1 tsp.	salt	5 mL
2 tbsp.	white vinegar	30 mL
1 cup	prepared horseradish	250 mL
1 cup	whipping cream, whipped	250 mL

- Dissolve gelatin in boiling water. Add salt, vinegar and horseradish. Chill until partially set.
- Fold in whipped cream. Pour into a 6-cup mold. Chill until set.

YIELD   **6-8 SERVINGS**

SPICED CRANBERRY MOLD

SUPERB WITH TURKEY OR ROAST PORK – BEAUTIFUL COLOR

3 oz.	pkg. cranberry gelatin	85 g
1 cup	boiling water	250 mL
½ cup	cold water	125 mL
¼ cup	blanched, slivered almonds	60 mL
1	apple, peeled, diced	1
½	celery stalk, chopped	½
¼ cup	whole-berry cranberry sauce	60 mL
¼ tsp.	ground cinnamon	1 mL
⅛ tsp.	ground cloves	0.5 mL

- Dissolve gelatin in boiling water. Stir in cold water. Chill until partially set.
- Combine remaining ingredients. Add to partially set gelatin. Pour into a 4-cup (1 L) mold. Chill until set.
- When set, unmold and garnish.

YIELD   **6 – 8 SERVINGS**

RHUBARB STRAWBERRY MOLD

VIVID ROSY COLOR AND GORGEOUS PRESENTATION

4 cups	chopped rhubarb	1 L
1 cup	water	250 mL
½ cup	sugar	125 mL
6 oz.	pkg. strawberry gelatin	170 g
1	orange, zest of	1
½ cup	orange juice	125 mL
1 cup	sliced fresh strawberries	250 mL
	lettuce leaves for garnish	
	strawberries for garnish	
	French vanilla OR strawberry yogurt	

- In a medium saucepan, over medium heat, cook and stir rhubarb, water and sugar until rhubarb is tender. Remove from heat.
- Stir in gelatin until dissolved. Add orange zest and juice. Chill until partially set. Stir in strawberries.
- Pour into a well-oiled 6-cup (1.5 L) ring mold. Refrigerate until set.
- Unmold onto a lettuce-lined tray and garnish with strawberries. Place yogurt in a small bowl that will fit in the center of the mold.

YIELD   *8 – 10 SERVINGS*

Commercial gelatin became widely available in the early 20th century. In the 1930s, flavored gelatin powders appeared, causing a great increase in the variety and availability of molded gelatin salads and desserts. Ginger ale was often added to created sparkling salads. When using fruit in gelatin preparations, it is important to know that raw papaya, kiwi and pineapple contain an enzyme that keeps the gelatin from setting. However, canned, or thoroughly cooked, these fruits may be used in gelatin salads and desserts.

Ambrosia Salad

LIGHT AND COLORFUL – AN OLD FAMILY FAVORITE AS A SALAD OR DESSERT

1 cup	sour cream	250 mL
10 oz.	can mandarin oranges, drained	284 mL
1 cup	pineapple tidbits, drained	250 mL
1 cup	miniature marshmallows	250 mL
1 cup	flaked coconut	250 mL
1 cup	green seedless grapes, halved	250 mL

- In a medium bowl, combine all ingredients.
- Refrigerate for 6 hours or overnight before serving.

YIELD   *6 SERVINGS*

Fresh Fruit Nestled in Barley

BARLEY ADDS NUTTY FLAVOR AND CHEWY TEXTURE TO THIS FRUIT SALAD

2 cups	cooked pearl barley	500 mL
1	apple, cored, diced	1
1	orange, peeled, chopped	1
1 cup	halved strawberries	250 mL
1 cup	seedless grapes	250 mL
1 cup	crushed pineapple	250 mL
2 tbsp.	brown sugar	30 mL
1 tbsp.	lemon juice	15 mL
	yogurt & mint leaves for garnish	

- In a large bowl, gently toss barley with fruit.
- Combine sugar and lemon juice. Gently stir into fruit. Chill for 4 hours.
- To serve, garnish with a dollop of yogurt and a sprig of mint leaves.

YIELD   *5 – 6 SERVINGS*

Apple, Raisin & Date Salad

HONEY, CINNAMON AND BANANA CREATE A LOVELY MELLOW DRESSING

Yogurt Banana Dressing:

½ cup	plain yogurt	125 mL
1	small banana, mashed	1
1 tbsp.	lemon juice	15 mL
1 tbsp.	liquid honey	15 mL
½ tsp.	ground cinnamon	2 mL
2	apples, peeled, cored, diced	2
¼ cup	raw sunflower seeds	60 mL
¼ cup	unsweetened flaked coconut	60 mL
½ cup	golden raisins	125 mL
½ cup	finely chopped dates	125 mL

- **For dressing**, blend all ingredients together.
- In a small bowl, combine salad ingredients. Pour dressing over; mix well.

VARIATIONS   *Carrot Apple Salad* – Substitute 2 cups (500 mL) grated carrots for 1 apple; substitute ¼ tsp. (1 mL) prepared mustard for the cinnamon.

YIELD   *6 SERVINGS*

 For over 5,000 years dates have been an important part of Middle Eastern and African cuisine. They also grow now in California and Arizona. Buy whole, unpitted, fresh or dried dates for the best quality. They should be plump and shiny, with no sugar crystals or mold on the surface. Sliced or chopped dates add sweetness and rich, deep flavor to meat and vegetable dishes, as well as to cereals, sandwiches and desserts. High in sugar and a good source of protein and iron, dates also make very good snacks for campers and hikers.

WILTED SPINACH SALAD

WARM BACON AND CIDER VINEGAR DRESSING – THIS IS BURSTING WITH FLAVOR

10 oz.	fresh spinach, washed, dried	283 g
1 tbsp.	bacon drippings	15 mL
1	small onion, chopped	1
2 tsp.	sugar	10 mL
½ tsp.	salt	2 mL
½ tsp.	dry mustard	2 mL
½ cup	cider vinegar	125 mL
	freshly ground pepper	
6 slices	bacon, cooked crisp, drained, crumbled	6 slices
3	hard-boiled eggs, peeled, chopped	3

- Place spinach in a large salad bowl.
- **For dressing**, in a skillet, heat bacon drippings and sauté onion until soft. Add sugar, salt, mustard and vinegar; continue to cook until sugar is dissolved. Pour hot dressing over spinach.
- Grind pepper over spinach and toss. Garnish with crumbled bacon and chopped eggs.

VARIATION   Omit the eggs and garnish with crumbled feta cheese and pitted ripe olives. Try red wine vinegar in place of cider vinegar. Also try crumbled blue cheese and chopped toasted pecans.

YIELD   *6 SERVINGS*

See photograph on page 67.

ORANGE-ALMOND LETTUCE SALAD

SUGARED ALMONDS AND ORANGES ACCENT FRESH VEGETABLES

¼ cup	sliced blanched almonds	60 mL
2 tsp.	sugar	10 mL
1 head	lettuce, torn into bite-sized pieces	1 head
3	radishes, sliced	3
3	green onions, chopped	3
2	celery stalks, chopped	2
¼	English cucumber, sliced	¼
10 oz.	can mandarin orange segments, drained, juice reserved	284 mL

GARLIC ORANGE DRESSING:

¼ cup	extra-virgin olive oil	60 mL
2 tbsp.	reserved orange juice	30 mL
1 tbsp.	sugar	15 mL
3 tbsp.	vinegar	45 mL
2	garlic cloves, minced	2
½ tsp.	salt	2 mL
¼ tsp.	pepper	1 mL

- In a small skillet, over low-medium heat, toast almonds in sugar until sugar melts and almonds are lightly browned. Cool. Set aside.
- In a large bowl, combine lettuce, other vegetables and orange segments.
- **For dressing**, place all ingredients in a blender. Process thoroughly. Pour dressing over vegetables; toss lightly.
- Serve salad sprinkled with toasted almonds.

YIELD   *6 – 8 SERVINGS*

JICAMA ORANGE SALAD

CRISP JICAMA HAS AN AFFINITY WITH ONIONS AND ORANGES

1	jicama, peeled, julienned	1
½	cucumber, peeled, halved lengthwise, thinly sliced	½
1	small red onion, thinly sliced	1
3	oranges, peeled, quartered, sliced	3
½ head	lettuce, in bite-sized pieces	½ head
¼ cup	vegetable oil	60 mL
3 tbsp.	rice vinegar	45 mL
½ tsp.	salt	2 mL
¼ tsp.	freshly ground pepper	1 mL

- In a large salad bowl, combine the first 5 ingredients.
- **For dressing**, in a small jar, combine remaining ingredients.
- When ready to serve, toss salad with dressing.

YIELD   *6 SERVINGS*

See photograph opposite.

Jicama, from Central and South America, looks like a flattened brown turnip. It has the crisp texture of a water chestnut, with a mild sweet, nutty flavor. It may be eaten raw or quickly sautéed, steamed, baked or boiled. To prepare, scrub, then peel and also remove the thin layer under the skin. Cut into slices, matchsticks or cubes. Citrus juices and hot pepper sauces complement the mild flavor of jicama.

MAIN COURSE – PORK

Pork Satay, page 145
Jicama Orange Salad, page 84

CARROT ORANGE SALAD

THIS WORKS — INTENSE COLOR AND GREAT FLAVOR

4 cups	grated carrots, about 8 carrots	1 L
1 cup	raisins OR chopped dates	250 mL
2-3	oranges, peeled, quartered, sliced	2-3
½ cup	mayonnaise	125 mL
3 tbsp.	orange juice	45 mL
2 tbsp.	lemon juice	30 mL
1 tbsp.	honey	15 mL
½ tsp.	salt	2 mL
¼-½ tsp.	cinnamon (optional)	1-2 mL

- In a medium bowl, combine grated carrots, raisins and orange slices.
- **For dressing**, combine remaining ingredients.
- Pour dressing over salad. Chill at least 1 hour before serving.

YIELD   6 – 8 SERVINGS

ORANGE ONION SALAD

SWEET AND SHARP — A DELICIOUS COMBINATION

2-3	oranges, peeled, quartered, sliced	2-3
½	sweet onion, finely chopped	½
½ cup	mayonnaise	125 mL
2 tbsp.	vinegar	30 mL
⅓ cup	sugar	75 mL
¼ cup	milk	60 mL
2 tbsp.	poppyseeds	30 mL
	lettuce OR spinach leaves	

- In a salad bowl, combine oranges and onion.
- **For dressing**, in a small bowl, combine mayonnaise, vinegar, sugar, milk and poppyseeds.
- Combine part of the dressing with the oranges and onion.
- Serve on a bed of lettuce or spinach. Refrigerate any remaining dressing.

YIELD   6 SERVINGS

ONION CUCUMBER SALAD

SOUR CREAM AND DILL ARE SUPERB WITH ONIONS AND CUCUMBERS

2	medium cucumbers, peeled, thinly sliced	2
1	large onion, peeled, thinly sliced	1
½ tsp	salt	2 mL
½ cup	sour cream OR plain yogurt	125 mL
1 tsp.	snipped fresh dill	5 mL
1 tbsp.	vinegar	15 mL
1 tbsp.	sugar	15 mL
¼ tsp.	pepper	1 mL
	greens – spinach, lettuce (optional)	

- A few hours before serving, place sliced vegetables in a colander in the sink. Sprinkle with salt. Let drain for at least an hour.
- **For dressing**, combine remaining ingredients, except greens.
- Transfer vegetables to a bowl. Add dressing and chill for at least an hour before serving to allow flavors to blend. Serve on a bed of greens.

YIELD   *6 – 8 SERVINGS*

MUSHROOMS & PEPPERS

CRUNCHY AND COLORFUL – GREAT FOR A BARBECUE OR PICNIC

2 cups	sliced mushrooms	500 mL
1	EACH red, yellow & green peppers, diced	1
3	green onions, chopped	3
1 tbsp.	chopped fresh parsley	15 mL
¼ cup	Superb French Dressing, see page 94	60 mL
	salt & pepper to taste	

- Place mushrooms, peppers and onions in a salad bowl.
- Combine parsley, dressing, salt and pepper; mix well.
- Gently toss dressing with vegetables. Serve.

YIELD   *6 SERVINGS*

SUNNY BROCCOLI SALAD

SO GOOD IT'S BECOME A CANADIAN CLASSIC

6 cups	broccoli florets	1.5 L
1 cup	golden raisins	250 mL
½	red onion, chopped	½
10 slices	bacon, cooked crisp, crumbled	10 slices
1 cup	raw sunflower seeds	250 mL
2 tbsp.	sugar	30 mL
½ cup	mayonnaise	125 mL
1 tbsp.	red wine vinegar	15 mL

- In a salad bowl, combine broccoli, raisins, onion, bacon and sunflower seeds.
- **For dressing**, in a small bowl, whisk together remaining ingredients. Toss with salad. Chill for several hours before serving.

YIELD   *8 SERVINGS*

CAULIFLOWER BROCCOLI SALAD

A HEALTHY, COLORFUL, CRISP, TAKE-ALONG SALAD

2 cups	EACH chopped broccoli & cauliflower	500 mL
½	red onion, chopped	½
½ cup	dried cranberries OR 1 cup (250 mL) halved green or red grapes	125 mL
⅓ cup	sunflower seeds	75 mL
2 tbsp.	toasted flax seeds	30 mL
⅓ cup	mayonnaise	75 mL
1 tbsp.	raspberry vinegar	15 mL
1 tbsp.	sugar	15 mL

- In a bowl, combine vegetables, cranberries and seeds.
- **For dressing**, blend the remaining ingredients. Toss with salad. Chill for several hours before serving.

YIELD   *6 SERVINGS*

LEBANESE BREAD SALAD

AN ADDICTIVE MIDDLE EASTERN TRADITION – TOASTED PITAS
BECOME TASTY CROÛTONS

½	English cucumber, diced	½
1	red pepper, thinly sliced	1
1 cup	thinly sliced green onion	250 mL
½ cup	sliced radishes	125 mL
1½ cups	coarsely chopped fresh parsley	375 mL
¼ cup	coarsely chopped fresh mint	60 mL
2	garlic cloves, crushed	2
½ tsp.	salt	2 mL
¼ cup	fresh lemon juice	60 mL
½ cup	olive oil	125 mL
¼ tsp.	EACH cinnamon & allspice	1 mL
	salt & pepper to taste	
2 cups	torn romaine lettuce (optional)	500 mL
3	tomatoes, diced	3
3-4	small pitas, opened, oven toasted, broken into bite-sized pieces	3-4

- In a salad bowl, combine cucumber, pepper, onion, radish, parsley and mint. Refrigerate until using.
- **For dressing**, in a small bowl, combine garlic, salt, lemon juice, oil and spices.
- To serve, add dressing to salad; mix well. Add romaine, tomatoes and pita; toss and serve.

YIELD   8 – 10 SERVINGS

See photograph on page 139.

COUSCOUS CHICKPEA SALAD

FRESH LEMON JUICE AND CUMIN MAKE A TANGY, EARTHY-TASTING DRESSING

1 tbsp.	butter	15 mL
3	garlic cloves, minced	3
1¼ cups	water	300 mL
1 cup	couscous	250 mL
½ tsp.	salt	2 mL
1 cup	chopped fresh parsley	250 mL
½	onion, finely chopped	½
2	Roma tomatoes, seeded, chopped	2
½	English cucumber, diced	½
2 cups	cooked chickpeas	500 mL
½ cup	crumbled feta cheese	125 mL
3 tbsp.	fresh lemon juice	45 mL
1½ tbsp.	olive oil	22 mL
1½ tsp.	ground cumin	7 mL
¾ tsp.	salt	4 mL
¼ tsp.	pepper	1 mL

- In a large saucepan, melt butter and sauté garlic. Add water; bring to a boil. Stir in couscous and salt. Remove from heat and cover. Let sit for 5 minutes, then stir with a fork. Cool.
- To couscous, add parsley, onion, tomatoes, cucumber, chickpeas and feta cheese.
- **For dressing**, combine lemon juice, oil, cumin, salt and pepper. Mix well. Toss lightly with couscous mixture.
- Refrigerate until ready to serve – up to 24 hours.

YIELD   *6 – 8 SERVINGS*

See photograph on page 121.

A north-African staple, couscous is a granular pasta made from semolina (crushed durum wheat). It may be served with meat, vegetables and fruit as a main dish, salad or dessert. It is also served with milk as a type of porridge.

PASTA AND FRESH VEGETABLE SALAD

PASTA SALADS ARE STAPLES AT BARBECUES AND PICNICS –
CIDER VINEGAR ADDS ZESTY FLAVOR

POPPY SEED DRESSING:

⅓ cup	sugar	75 mL
1 tsp.	salt	5 mL
⅓ cup	apple cider vinegar	75 mL
½	onion, chopped	½
2 tbsp.	poppy seeds	30 mL
⅔ cup	vegetable oil	150 mL
4 cups	cooked pasta (rotini, fusilli, macaroni)	1 L
1	red OR green pepper, chopped	1
2	carrots, thinly sliced	2
4	green onions, chopped	4
½	English cucumber, sliced	½
2 cups	chopped broccoli florets	500 mL
1 cup	grated Cheddar cheese	250 mL

- **For dressing**, in a blender, combine sugar, salt, vinegar, onion and poppy seeds. With the blender running, slowly pour in oil; blend thoroughly
- In a large bowl, combine pasta, pepper, carrots, onion, cucumber and broccoli.
- Pour dressing over pasta and vegetables. Refrigerate for several hours or overnight.
- Just before serving, toss the cheese with the salad.

NOTE   Let pasta salads come to room temperature before serving. Taste and adjust the seasoning as the pasta (starch) absorbs flavors, sometimes making the salad too bland.

YIELD   *6 SERVINGS*

PASTA PERFECTION

MEDITERRANEAN FLAVORS ARE PERFECT IN PASTA SALAD

1½ cups	dry small pasta (rotini, fusilli, etc.)	375 mL
2 tbsp.	olive oil	30 mL
1	head of broccoli, cut into florets	1
½	green OR red pepper, diced	½
1	garlic clove, minced	1
10-12	grape tomatoes	10-12
10-12	kalamata olives, pitted, chopped	10-12
3 tbsp.	extra-virgin olive oil	45 mL
2 tbsp.	red wine vinegar	30 mL
1 tsp.	dried basil	5 mL
⅓ cup	grated Parmesan cheese	75 mL
	freshly ground pepper	

- Cook pasta to "al dente" stage according to package directions. Drain, rinse and cool.
- In a skillet over medium-high heat, heat 2 tbsp. (30 mL) oil and sauté broccoli, pepper and garlic until broccoli is tender-crisp, 3-4 minutes.
- In a large bowl, combine pasta, sautéed vegetables, tomatoes and olives.
- **For dressing**, combine 3 tbsp. (45 mL) oil, vinegar and basil. Pour over salad; toss well. Toss Parmesan with salad. Add freshly ground pepper to taste.
- Serve immediately or refrigerate to serve later.

YIELD   8 SERVINGS

24-Hour Barbecue Coleslaw

A great make-ahead salad – can you have a barbecue without coleslaw?

1	large head cabbage, shredded	1
1	green pepper, chopped	1
1	onion, sliced into rings	1
1 cup	sugar	250 mL
1 cup	vinegar	250 mL
¾ cup	vegetable oil	175 mL
1 tbsp.	EACH sugar, celery seed, salt & dry mustard	15 mL

- Layer cabbage, green pepper and onion rings in a container with a tight-fitting lid. Sprinkle with sugar. Do NOT stir.
- In a small saucepan, bring vinegar, oil, remaining sugar, celery seed, salt and dry mustard to the boiling point. Remove from heat; pour over layered vegetables. Do NOT stir.
- Chill, tightly covered, for at least 24 hours. Mix well before serving.
- Refrigerated, this salad will keep well for a few days.

YIELD   *10 – 12 SERVINGS*

Superb French Dressing

Tangy and sweet – the name says it all

1 cup	ketchup	250 mL
¼ cup	sugar	60 mL
½ cup	herb-flavored vinegar	125 mL
1 tsp.	salt	5 mL
1	small onion, quartered	1
2	garlic cloves, peeled	2
½ tsp.	celery seed	2 mL
¼ tsp.	paprika	1 mL
¾ cup	olive OR vegetable oil	175 mL

- Place all ingredients in a blender; blend for 1 minute.

YIELD   *3 CUPS (750 ML)*

Thousand Island Dressing

NOW YOU CAN MAKE THIS MUCH-LOVED DRESSING AT HOME

1 cup	mayonnaise	250 mL
2 tbsp.	chopped onion	30 mL
¾ cup	diced celery	175 mL
¼ cup	EACH stuffed olives, sweet pickle relish & chili sauce	60 mL
3 sprigs	fresh parsley	3 sprigs
2 tbsp.	chopped green pepper	30 mL
1	hard-boiled egg, quartered (optional)	1
1 tsp.	paprika	5 mL
	salt & pepper to taste	

• Place all ingredients in a blender. Blend until solids are finely chopped.

YIELD   *3½ CUPS (875 ML)*

Apple Chutney

SWEET AND SPICY – GREAT WITH ROAST PORK OR GAME

1 tsp.	pickling salt	5 mL
2 cups	brown sugar	500 mL
2 cups	white vinegar	500 mL
6	apples, peeled, chopped	6
2 cups	raisins	500 mL
1	medium onion, chopped	1
½	red pepper, chopped	½
2 tbsp.	mustard seed	30 mL
1 tbsp.	freshly grated ginger	15 mL
1 tsp.	ground allspice	5 mL
1	hot red chili pepper, finely chopped	1
1	garlic clove, minced	1

• In a large saucepan, over low heat, dissolve salt and sugar in vinegar.
• Add remaining ingredients. Cook slowly until tender, about 45 minutes. Pour into hot sterilized jars and seal.

YIELD   *6 CUPS (1.5 L)*

BEET PICKLES IN A PAIL

COLORFUL, TASTY AND OH SO EASY TO MAKE

8 cups	cooked, sliced beets	2 L
2 cups	sugar	500 mL
1 cup	EACH vinegar & water	250 mL
½ tsp.	EACH celery seed, turmeric & dry mustard	2 mL
2 tsp.	pickling salt	10 mL
1 tbsp.	mixed pickling spice, tied in cheesecloth	15 mL

- Place cooked beets in a 2-quart (2 L) pail.
- **For brine**, in a large saucepan, combine remaining ingredients. Bring to a boil; reduce heat and simmer for 15 minutes. Remove spice bag.
- Pour hot brine over beets in pail. Leave at room temperature until cool.
- Refrigerate for 2 weeks to allow flavors to develop. Serve as desired.

YIELD   2 QUARTS (2 L)

SWEET PUMPKIN PICKLES

SWEET AND GINGERY – SERVE WITH THANKSGIVING TURKEY OR PORK

2 cups	cider vinegar	500 mL
3 lbs.	sugar	1.5 kg
1 tsp.	whole cloves	5 mL
1 tbsp.	crushed cinnamon stick	15 mL
3 slices	fresh ginger OR 2 pieces crystallized	3 slices
6 lbs.	pumpkin, peeled, in 1" (2.5 cm) cubes	2.5 kg

- In a large heavy saucepan, bring vinegar and sugar to a boil, stirring until sugar is dissolved. Tie cloves, cinnamon and ginger in cheesecloth. Add to saucepan and boil for 5 minutes.
- Add pumpkin; bring to a rolling boil, then reduce heat and simmer, stirring often, for 25 minutes. Remove spice bag.
- Place pumpkin in hot sterilized jars; pour vinegar syrup into jars to cover pumpkin. Seal jars.

YIELD   7 – 8 PINTS (7 – 8, 500 ML JARS)

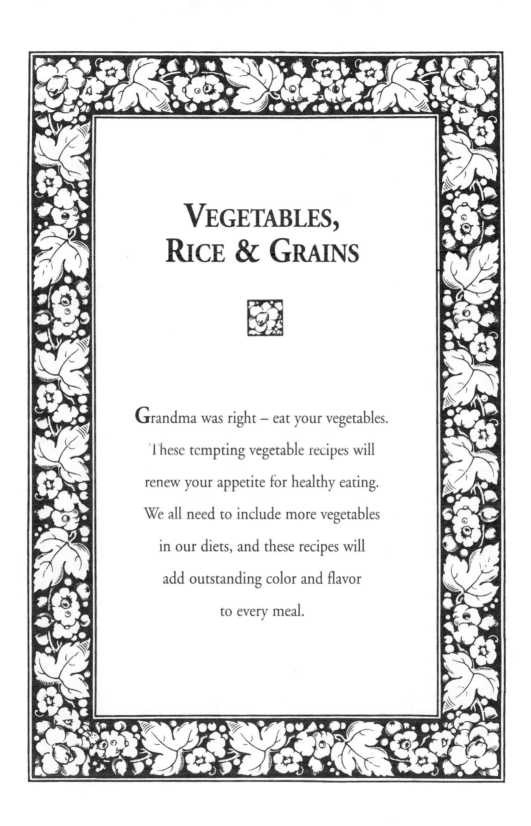

VEGETABLES, RICE & GRAINS

Grandma was right – eat your vegetables.
These tempting vegetable recipes will
renew your appetite for healthy eating.
We all need to include more vegetables
in our diets, and these recipes will
add outstanding color and flavor
to every meal.

FRIED GREEN TOMATOES

A SOUTHERN TRADITION – REMEMBER THE MOVIE!

2 cups	yellow cornmeal OR flour	500 mL
1 tbsp.	EACH chopped fresh parsley & thyme (optional)	15 mL
	salt & pepper to taste	
4	large green tomatoes, sliced	4
	vegetable or olive oil for frying	

- In a shallow plate, combine cornmeal and seasonings. Dredge tomato slices in cornmeal mixture.
- In a skillet, heat a small amount of oil over medium heat. Add tomatoes, a few at a time, and fry until crisp and golden, turning to fry both sides. Add oil as needed.
- Drain on paper towels and serve hot, as is or with a tomato salsa.

YIELD   *4 SERVINGS*

GARLICKY CHERRY TOMATOES

TANTALIZING AROMA – WONDERFUL COLOR AND FLAVOR

2 tbsp.	olive oil OR butter	30 mL
2	green onions, sliced	2
2	garlic cloves, crushed	2
4 cups	cherry tomatoes	1 L
1 tbsp.	EACH chopped fresh parsley, basil, & thyme	15 mL
	salt & pepper to taste	

- In a large skillet, heat oil. Add onion and garlic; cook for 2-3 minutes.
- Add tomatoes to pan, cook over medium heat for 4-5 minutes, stirring gently. Remove from heat and sprinkle with herbs and seasonings.

YIELD   *4 – 5 SERVINGS*

See photograph on page 103.

BLUE CHEESE BROILED TOMATOES

SIMPLY SUMPTUOUS!

6	ripe tomatoes, halved	6
6 oz.	blue cheese, crumbed	115 g
3-4 tsp.	chopped fresh oregano	15-20 mL
	salt, pepper & olive oil to taste	

- Place tomato halves in oiled, shallow baking pan, cut side up. Top with cheese, oregano, salt and pepper. Drizzle with olive oil.
- Broil for 6-7 minutes, or until cheese starts to brown.

YIELD   *12 TOMATO HALVES*

RATATOUILLE STIR-FRY

A COLORFUL MEDITERRANEAN DISH – GOOD HOT OR COLD!

2 tbsp.	vegetable oil	30 mL
½	medium onion, sliced	½
2	garlic cloves, minced	2
6	mushrooms, sliced	6
½	EACH green & orange pepper, chopped	½
½	small zucchini, sliced	½
½	eggplant, unpeeled, cubed	½
1	Roma tomato, diced	1
½ tsp.	Italian seasoning	2 mL
	salt & freshly ground pepper	

- In a skillet, over medium-high heat, heat oil. Add onion, garlic, mushrooms, peppers, zucchini and eggplant. Stir-fry for 4 minutes, until tender.
- Reduce heat to a simmer. Add tomato and seasonings. Continue to cook until tomato has softened, about 1 minute.

YIELD   *4 SERVINGS*

SUNNY DAY CARROTS

CARROTS IN A BUTTERY CITRUS GLAZE

8	medium carrots, sliced	8
1 tbsp.	sugar	15 mL
¼ tsp.	salt	1 mL
2 tsp.	cornstarch	10 mL
1 tsp.	grated lemon zest	5 mL
1 tbsp.	lemon juice	15 mL
⅔ cup	orange juice	150 mL
2 tbsp.	butter	30 mL

- In a large saucepan, boil carrots in water to cover for 4-6 minutes; OR cook, covered, in a steamer over boiling water for 7-10 minutes, just until tender.
- In a separate saucepan, combine sugar, salt, cornstarch and lemon zest. Stir in lemon juice, orange juice and butter; heat until thickened and bubbly.
- Add carrots to sauce. Serve warm.

YIELD   *6 – 8 SERVINGS*

BROCCOLI CARROT CASSEROLE

ZESTY FLAVOR AND GORGEOUS COLOR

1	large broccoli head, cut into florets	1
4	carrots, thinly sliced	4
2	Spanish onions, sliced	2
1 cup	dry white wine	250 mL
⅔ cup	Italian dressing	150 mL
½ cup	bread crumbs	125 mL
2 tbsp.	melted butter	30 mL
	salt & pepper to taste	

BROCCOLI CARROT CASSEROLE

(CONTINUED)

- In a 3-quart (3 L), lightly greased casserole, combine broccoli, carrots and onions. Combine wine and Italian dressing; pour over vegetables.
- Combine crumbs, butter, salt and pepper. Sprinkle over vegetables.
- Bake, covered, at 350°F (180°C) for 30 minutes. Uncover and bake until vegetables are tender, about 25 minutes.

YIELD   8 SERVINGS

GREEN BEAN CASSEROLE

CREAMY SAUCE AND CRUNCHY TOPPING

1 lb.	fresh green beans	450 g
2 tbsp.	butter, divided	30 mL
1 tbsp.	all-purpose flour	15 mL
½ tsp.	EACH sugar & salt	2 mL
⅛ tsp.	pepper	0.5 mL
¼ cup	milk	60 mL
¼	onion, finely chopped	¼
½ cup	sour cream	125 mL
3 oz.	Swiss cheese, grated	85 g
½ cup	Special K cereal	125 mL

- Trim ends off beans; cut into 1" (2.5 cm) lengths. Steam beans until tender crisp. Rinse in cold water.
- In a saucepan, over medium heat, melt 1 tbsp. (15 mL) butter. Blend in flour, sugar, salt and pepper. Stir in milk; cook until thickened. Remove from heat.
- Add onion and sour cream to sauce. Stir in beans and grated cheese. Transfer beans to a buttered 1½-quart (1.5 L) casserole.
- Combine cereal and 1 tbsp. (15 mL) butter. Sprinkle over beans.
- Bake, uncovered, at 400°F (200°C) for 15 minutes, or until hot.

YIELD   6 SERVINGS

TENDER-CRISP CHINESE VEGETABLES

USE YOUR FAVORITE VEGETABLES – THIS DISH IS VERY VERSATILE

1 tbsp.	vegetable oil	15 mL
1	celery stalk, chopped	1
1	red OR green pepper, chopped	1
½	onion, sliced	½
1	garlic clove, minced	1
8	mushrooms, sliced	8
½ cup	chicken stock	125 mL
2 tbsp.	soy sauce	30 mL
1 cup	bean sprouts	250 mL
20	pea pods	20
½	Chinese cabbage, shredded	½
2 tbsp.	cornstarch	30 mL
3 tbsp.	cold water	45 mL

- In a wok or skillet, over high heat, heat oil. Add celery, pepper, onion, garlic and mushrooms. Stir-fry for 3 minutes.
- Combine stock and soy sauce. Add to wok with sprouts, pea pods and cabbage.
- Mix cornstarch and water to a smooth paste. Add to vegetables. Stir constantly for 2-3 minutes, or until sauce thickens and vegetables are just tender crisp. Serve immediately.

VARIATIONS   To make this a one-wok dinner, add 2 cups (500 mL) shrimp or strips of chicken, pork or beef. For cooked seafood or meats, just stir-fry until heated through; for raw, stir-fry before the vegetable, then set aside and reheat when adding cornstarch.

YIELD   *4 SERVINGS*

MAIN COURSE – SEAFOOD

Szechuan Shrimp, page 118
Garlicky Cherry Tomatoes, page 98

DEVILED CORN

JUST SLIGHTLY DEVILED – A REAL DEVIL MIGHT ADD A DASH
OR TWO OF HOT PEPPER SAUCE!

¼ cup	butter	60 mL
2 tbsp.	all-purpose flour	30 mL
1 tsp.	prepared mustard	5 mL
½ tsp.	Worcestershire sauce	2 mL
1 tbsp.	lemon juice	15 mL
½ tsp.	salt	2 mL
¼ tsp.	pepper	1 mL
½ cup	milk	125 mL
4 slices	bacon, cooked, drained, crumbled	4 slices
14 oz.	can whole-kernel corn	398 mL
14 oz.	can cream-style corn	398 mL
½ cup	grated Parmesan cheese	125 mL
½ cup	fine cracker crumbs	125 mL
1 tbsp.	butter, melted	15 mL
4	hard-boiled eggs for garnish	4
	olives for garnish	

- In a saucepan, melt ¼ cup (60 mL) butter; stir in flour, mustard, Worcestershire sauce, lemon juice, salt and pepper. Add milk all at once. Cook, stirring, until thick and bubbly. Remove from heat.
- Stir in bacon, whole-kernel corn and cream-style corn.
- Spoon mixture into a lightly greased 1½-quart (1.5 L) casserole. Sprinkle with cheese. Combine crumbs and melted butter; sprinkle over cheese.
- Bake at 350°F (180°C) for 45 minutes, or until heated through. Garnish with hard-boiled egg wedges and olive slices.

YIELD   *8 SERVINGS*

HARVARD BEETS

APPLE CIDER VINEGAR ADDS TART FLAVOR

2 tbsp.	sugar	30 mL
1 tbsp.	cornstarch	15 mL
½ tsp.	salt	2 mL
¾ cup	water	175 mL
¼ cup	apple cider vinegar	60 mL
1 lb.	beets, cooked, peeled, sliced	500 g
2 tbsp.	butter	30 mL

- In a saucepan, combine sugar, cornstarch and salt. Gradually stir in water and vinegar. Bring to a rapid boil; cook for 3 minutes.
- Add beets and butter; return to a boil. Cover; simmer 10 minutes. Serve hot.

VARIATION   Add ½ onion and 2 apples, chopped and sautéed.

YIELD   **6 SERVINGS**

ROASTED ROOT VEGETABLE MEDLEY

ROASTING CREATES A RICH CARAMEL FLAVOR

3	potatoes	3
4	EACH carrots & parsnips	4
1	sweet potato	1
1	rutabaga (Swedish turnip)	1
2	onions, quartered	2
4	garlic cloves (optional)	4
¼ cup	olive oil	60 mL
1 tsp.	salt	5 mL
¼ tsp.	pepper	1 mL
	chopped rosemary, sage, parsley, savory OR thyme (optional)	

ROASTED ROOT VEGETABLE MEDLEY

(CONTINUED)

- Peel vegetables; cut into appropriate-sized pieces for baking. Carrots and parsnips require the most time to cook so those pieces should be smaller than potatoes, yams and rutabagas.
- Place vegetable pieces in a plastic bag.
- Add oil to thoroughly coat all vegetables when mixed in the bag.
- Place oiled vegetables in a shallow, greased 9 x 13" (23 x 33 cm) baking pan. Sprinkle with salt and pepper.
- Bake at 350°F (180°C) for 45-60 minutes, turning vegetables frequently, until tender. To serve, sprinkle with desired herbs.

VARIATION   Also try adding squash, turnips, leeks, fennel bulbs and celery root.

YIELD   *6 SERVINGS*

ROASTED GARLIC

SUCCULENT, AND WHAT AN AROMA!

3	whole garlic heads	3
¼ cup	chicken stock	60 mL
3 tbsp.	olive oil	45 mL
½ tsp.	EACH salt & pepper	2 mL

- Remove papery outer skins of garlic heads; leave cloves intact.
- Cut a slice off the top of each head just to expose individual cloves.
- Arrange garlic heads in a small baking dish. Pour in stock. Sprinkle oil, salt and pepper over garlic heads. Cover securely.
- Bake at 350°F (180°C) for an hour, or until cloves are golden brown.
- Squeeze baked cloves onto French baguettes slices; or add to freshly mashed potatoes.

YIELD   *24 – 30 BAKED GARLIC CLOVES*

TWICE-BAKED POTATOES

CAN BE PREPARED IN ADVANCE, REFRIGERATED AND REHEATED

4	baking potatoes	4
⅓ cup	milk	75 mL
2 tbsp.	butter, softened	30 mL
	salt & pepper to taste	
4 oz.	Cheddar cheese, grated	115 g
1 tbsp.	chopped fresh chives	15 mL
	paprika	
	sour cream & crisp, crumbled bacon	

• Bake potatoes until tender. Let cool until easy to handle. Cut tops off lengthwise. Gently scoop out potatoes, leaving a ½" (1 cm) shell.
• Mash scooped-out flesh with milk, butter, salt and pepper. Beat until light and fluffy. Stir in cheese and chives. Fill potato shells with stuffing mixture. Place on an ungreased baking dish. Sprinkle with paprika.
• Reheat at 400°F (200°C) for 20 minutes, or until thoroughly heated.
• If desired, serve with sour cream and bacon.

VARIATION   For a low-fat version, mix potato flesh with 8 oz. non-fat plain yogurt, dry onion soup mix and 3 tbsp. (45 mL) skim milk.

YIELD   *4 SERVINGS*

OVEN-BAKED BACON CHEDDAR POTATOES

A CRISPY GOLDEN CHEDDAR TOPPING

6	medium potatoes, peeled, grated	6
1	onion, chopped	1
1 cup	creamed cottage cheese	250 mL
1	egg, beaten	1
1 tbsp.	flour	15 mL
	salt & pepper to taste	
6 slices	bacon, cooked, crumbled	6 slices
½ cup	grated Cheddar cheese	125 mL

OVEN-BAKED BACON CHEDDAR POTATOES
(CONTINUED)

- In a large bowl, combine potatoes, onion, cottage cheese, egg, flour, salt and pepper.
- Pour into a lightly greased 9 x 13" (23 x 33 cm) casserole or baking pan.
- Bake at 350°F (180°C) for 45 minutes.
- Sprinkle bacon and cheese over potatoes. Bake for 15 minutes. or until cheese is melted.

YIELD   *6 SERVINGS*

CHEDDAR SCALLOPED POTATOES
VERY TRADITIONAL – WONDERFUL WITH BAKED HAM

6 tbsp.	butter, divided	90 mL
1½ cups	thinly sliced onion	375 mL
¼ cup	flour	60 mL
3 cups	milk, scalded	750 mL
	salt & pepper to taste	
¼ tsp.	nutmeg	1 mL
2 lbs.	potatoes, very thinly sliced	1 kg
1½ cups	grated old Cheddar cheese	375 mL
½ cup	dry bread crumbs	125 mL

- In a skillet, melt 2 tbsp. (30 mL) butter. Add onion; cook until soft.
- In a small saucepan, over medium heat, melt remaining butter; stir in flour. Cook, stirring, for 2-3 minutes. Gradually whisk in milk; cook and stir until thickened, about 2 minutes. Add salt, pepper and nutmeg.
- Pour ⅓ of sauce into a buttered 3-quart (3 L) casserole. Layer ⅓ of potatoes, overlapping slices; layer ½ of onions, then ⅓ of cheese. Repeat layers twice, using all of the sauce, potatoes and cheese.
- Sprinkle with crumbs; dot with additional butter if you wish. Bake at 400°F (200°C), covered, for 30 minutes. Uncover and bake for 35-45 minutes more, until potatoes are tender. Lower heat to 350°F (180°C) if top browns too much or cover casserole again.

VARIATIONS   Substitute chicken stock for milk. Add 2 cloves crushed garlic and a splash of hot pepper sauce. Try Swiss, Gruyère or Parmesan cheese instead of Cheddar.

YIELD   *6 – 8 SERVINGS*

CAJUN RICE

SWEET, SPICY AND SATISFYING – THIS IS THE FAMOUS SOUTHERN DIRTY RICE

2 tbsp.	olive oil	30 mL
1 tbsp.	all-purpose flour	15 mL
1	large onion, chopped	1
4	garlic cloves, minced	4
½ cup	apple juice	125 mL
½	sweet potato, diced	½
½	red pepper, diced	½
½	green pepper, diced	½
1	carrot, diced	1
1	celery stalk, chopped	1
1½ cups	long-grain white rice	375 mL
3 cups	chicken stock	750 mL
½ tsp.	salt	2 mL
¼ tsp.	cayenne pepper, or to taste	1 mL
½ tsp.	black pepper	2 mL

- In a large sauté pan, combine oil and flour. Cook and stir over medium heat for 2 minutes.
- Add onion, garlic and apple juice; cook and stir until onion is soft and browned.
- Add sweet potato, peppers, carrot and celery. Cook and stir for 4 minutes. Add rice; cook and stir for a minute.
- Add chicken stock; bring to a boil. Reduce heat; cover and cook, stirring occasionally, for 20 minutes, or until liquid is absorbed and rice is tender. Add seasonings to taste. Serve hot.

YIELD   *6 – 8 SERVINGS*

RISOTTO WITH SPINACH AND GORGONZOLA

THE SECRET TO A GREAT RISOTTO IS GRADUALLY STIRRING IN THE HOT STOCK,
UNTIL IT IS COMPLETELY ABSORBED, BEFORE ADDING MORE STOCK

2 cups	chicken stock	500 mL
1 tbsp.	olive oil	15 mL
2	garlic cloves, minced	2
½	onion, chopped	½
1 cup	arborio rice	250 mL
¼ cup	white wine	60 mL
4 oz.	fresh baby spinach	115 g
3 oz.	gorgonzola cheese, crumbled	85 g
	salt & freshly ground pepper	

- In a small saucepan, bring stock to a boil. Reduce to a simmer.
- In a large saucepan, heat oil. Add garlic and onion; cook until soft.
- Add rice; stir to coat. Add wine to rice; cook and stir until wine is absorbed.
- Add stock, ¼-½ cup (60-125 mL) at a time, stirring until liquid is absorbed before adding more. Continue until all stock is used and rice is cooked.
- Add spinach, cheese and seasonings. Stir until spinach is wilted and cheese has melted. Serve immediately.

VARIATIONS   For **Lemon Risotto**, omit gorgonzola and add juice and grated zest of 1 lemon, plus ¼ cup (60 mL) grated Parmesan cheese.

For **Risotto Milanese**, omit spinach and gorgonzola, add 1 generous pinch of saffron to chicken stock. Gently stir ½ cup (125 mL) grated Parmesan cheese into cooked rice.

For **Seafood Risotto**, add chopped, sautéed fish and/or shellfish to Risotto Milanese. Omit the Parmesan and add minced chives.

YIELD   *3 – 4 SERVINGS*

SPANISH RICE

BROWN RICE MAKES THIS FAVORITE DISH MORE NUTRITIOUS

½	EACH green pepper & onion, chopped	½
2	cloves garlic, minced	2
1 cup	brown rice	250 mL
2 tsp.	vegetable oil	10 mL
19 oz.	can spicy red pepper chunky tomatoes OR stewed tomatoes, NOT drained	540 mL
¼ cup	water	60 mL
2 tbsp.	red wine vinegar	30 mL
	salt & pepper to taste	
3¾ oz.	Monterey Jack cheese, shredded	100 g

- In a heavy-bottomed saucepan, heat oil; sauté pepper, onion, garlic and rice for 3-4 minutes.
- Add tomatoes, water and vinegar. Bring to a boil; reduce heat to simmer. Cook, covered, for 40 minutes, or until rice is tender.
- If desired, adjust seasoning with salt and pepper.
- Sprinkle cheese over rice. Serve as soon as cheese is melted.

YIELD   *8 SERVINGS*

GREEK RICE

FETA, GREEK OLIVES AND HERBS – A CLASSIC!

2 cups	water OR chicken stock	500 mL
½ tsp.	salt	2 mL
2	garlic cloves, minced	2
2 tsp.	olive oil	10 mL
1 cup	long-grain white rice	250 mL
3	green onions, chopped	3
¼ cup	chopped Greek black olives	60 mL
3 oz.	feta cheese, crumbled	85 g
½ tsp.	EACH dried oregano & rosemary	2 mL
¼ tsp.	ground thyme	1 mL
1 cup	chopped Roma tomatoes (optional)	250 mL

GREEK RICE

(CONTINUED)

- In a medium saucepan, bring water, salt, garlic and oil to a boil. Add rice; return to a boil. Reduce heat, cover and simmer until rice is tender and liquid is absorbed, about 20 minutes. Remove from heat.
- Stir in remaining ingredients. Serve hot.

VARIATION   Stir 2 cups (500 mL) shredded spinach into hot rice during last 2 minutes of cooking.

YIELD   *5 – 6 SERVINGS*

MAPLE HAM & MUSHROOM WILD RICE

HIGHLIGHTS THE NUTTY FLAVOR AND CHEWY TEXTURE OF WILD RICE

1 cup	wild rice	250 mL
¼ tsp.	salt	1 mL
3 cups	boiling water	750 mL
2 tbsp.	vegetable oil	30 mL
6 slices	smoked maple ham, chopped	6 slices
1	onion, chopped	1
1	celery stalk, chopped	1
1½ cups	sliced mushrooms	375 mL
4 oz.	old Cheddar cheese, grated	115 g
14 oz.	can diced tomatoes	398 mL
⅔ cup	hot water	150 mL

- In a medium saucepan, combine rice, salt and boiling water. Simmer for 30 minutes, or until rice is tender; drain.
- In a skillet, heat oil; cook ham, onion and celery until vegetables are tender. Add mushrooms; cook until tender.
- Combine rice, cooked vegetables, cheese, tomatoes and water. Place in a buttered 2-quart (2 L) casserole.
- Bake, covered, at 350°F (180°C) for 1 hour.

YIELD   *8 SERVINGS*

ORZO, BARLEY & MUSHROOMS

THE NUTTY TOASTED FLAVOR OF BARLEY IS GREAT WITH MUSHROOMS

1 cup	fresh sliced mushrooms	250 mL
4	green onions, chopped	4
2 tbsp.	butter	30 mL
½ cup	EACH orzo & pearl barley	125 mL
1 cup	beef stock	250 mL
1½ cups	water	375 mL
	salt & pepper to taste	

- In a large heavy saucepan, melt butter; sauté mushrooms and onions until tender. Add orzo and barley; stir until golden brown.
- Add stock and water; bring to a boil. Reduce heat to low; cook for 30 minutes, or until liquid is absorbed. Season, toss and serve.

YIELD   4 SERVINGS

BUCKWHEAT CASSEROLE

BUCKWHEAT (KASHA) IS IRRESISTIBLE – HERE IS ANOTHER DELICIOUS OPTION

1 tbsp.	butter	15 mL
1	medium onion, chopped	1
2 cups	water	500 mL
	salt & pepper to taste	
1 cup	buckwheat seeds, rinsed	250 mL
½ lb.	bacon, cooked crisp, crumbled	250 g
3 cups	sauerkraut, rinsed	750 mL
2 cups	crushed OR diced tomatoes	500 mL

- In a large saucepan, melt butter; sauté onion until translucent. Add water, salt, pepper and buckwheat. Bring to a boil. Simmer for 15 minutes, stirring occasionally. Remove from heat. Add bacon, sauerkraut and tomatoes.
- Transfer buckwheat to a lightly greased 2½-quart (2.5 L) casserole.
- Bake, covered, at 325°F (160°C) for 1 hour, or until buckwheat is tender.

YIELD   6 – 8 SERVINGS

Main Courses

Familiar or exotic, these traditional recipes, from grandmas of many cultures, are true comfort food. Satisfying flavors and tantalizing aromas make these main-dish recipes family favorites. Suggested variations also inspire creative adaptations.

GRILLED WALLEYE

WALLEYE, PICKEREL, PIKE-PERCH – THEY'RE ALL THE SAME AND ALL ARE DELICIOUS

1 tbsp.	butter, softened	15 mL
1½ lbs.	walleye OR other firm white fish fillets	675 g
1 tbsp.	lemon juice	15 mL
1 tbsp.	chopped fresh basil	15 mL
1 tsp.	lemon pepper seasoning	5 mL
1	garlic clove, minced	1
½ tsp.	salt	2 mL
6	mushrooms, sliced	6

- Lightly butter a large piece of foil wrap. Place fillets in center of foil. Spread with remaining butter.
- Sprinkle fillets with lemon juice, basil, lemon pepper, garlic and salt. Layer mushroom slices on top. Fold foil edges together to seal tightly.
- Place foil packet on hot grill, turning once, for 10-15 minutes, or until fillets flake easily with a fork.

YIELD   5 – 6 SERVINGS

HALIBUT WITH SESAME SEEDS

MILD-FLAVORED HALIBUT SHINES WITH A CRUNCHY SESAME COATING

⅓ cup	rice vinegar	75 mL
½ cup	soy sauce	125 mL
1 tbsp.	sugar	15 mL
1 tsp.	ground ginger	5 mL
2	garlic cloves, minced	2
pinch	cayenne pepper	pinch
4 x 6 oz.	halibut fillets	4 x 170 g
	sesame seeds	
	vegetable oil	

HALIBUT WITH SESAME SEEDS

(CONTINUED)

- In a small saucepan, combine vinegar, soy sauce, sugar, ginger, garlic and cayenne; bring to a boil. Reduce heat; simmer for 5 minutes. Set aside.
- Place halibut fillets in a shallow pan. Brush both sides with hot soy sauce mixture; let sit 15 minutes.
- Place sesame seeds in a shallow dish. Coat fillets with seeds.
- In a skillet, over medium heat, heat oil. Cook fillets, 3-4 minutes per side, or until browned.
- Return soy sauce to heat; bring to a boil. Boil 5 minutes to reduce. Remove from heat; keep warm. Serve fillets brushed with reduced sauce.

YIELD   *4 SERVINGS*

MARINATED BAKED SALMON

THE RUB BAKES TO A SPICY SWEET GLAZE

2-3 lb.	salmon fillet	1-1.5 kg

MARINATING DRY RUB:

½ cup	brown sugar	125 mL
1 tbsp.	EACH salt & white pepper	15 mL
1 tbsp.	EACH nutmeg & allspice	15 mL

- With a knife, score salmon fillet, lengthwise and crosswise at about 2" (5 cm) intervals.
- Combine rub ingredients. Rub over salmon. Marinate for 4 hours in refrigerator or 1 hour at room temperature.
- Bake at 375°F (190°C), or barbecue on low to medium heat, for 15 to 20 minutes (10 minutes per 1" [2.5 cm] of thickness), or until fillet flakes.

VARIATION   ***Cedar Planked Salmon*** – Soak an 8 x 12" (20 x 30 cm) non-treated cedar plank in water for several hours. Bake or barbecue salmon on plank as above.

YIELD   *6 – 8 SERVINGS*

SZECHUAN SHRIMP

SUCCULENT SHRIMP WITH A FIERY SAUCE

SZECHUAN SAUCE:

1 tbsp.	tomato paste	15 mL
2 tsp.	chili bean sauce OR Chinese Chili sauce	10 mL
2 tsp.	cider vinegar	10 mL
½ tsp.	EACH salt & pepper	2 mL
2 tsp.	EACH sugar & sesame oil	10 mL
2 tbsp.	vegetable oil	30 mL
1 tbsp.	minced gingerroot	15 mL
2-3	garlic cloves, crushed	2-3
3 tbsp.	chopped green onion	45 mL
1 lb.	raw, peeled, deveined shrimp	500 g
	chopped green onion for garnish	

- In a small bowl, combine all sauce ingredients; set aside.
- In a wok, over high heat, heat oil. Add ginger, garlic and green onions. Stir-fry for 30 seconds; add shrimp and stir-fry for 1-2 minutes.
- Add sauce to shrimp and stir-fry for 2-3 minutes. Garnish.

YIELD   *4 SERVINGS*

See photograph on page 103.

CHILI LIME SAUCE

GREAT WITH SHRIMP, GREEN ONION CAKES, PAGE 52, SPRING ROLLS, CHICKEN

1	garlic clove	1
1 tsp.	dried red chili flakes, or to taste	5 mL
2 tbsp.	sugar, or more, to taste	30 mL
⅓ cup	soy sauce	75 mL
2½ tbsp.	fresh lime juice	37 mL
¼ cup	chicken stock OR water	60 mL
1 tsp.	grated fresh ginger	5 mL

- Blend all ingredients until smooth. Cover; refrigerate until using.

YIELDS   *ABOUT ¾ CUP (175 ML)*

Coq au Vin

A SIMPLE VERSION OF THE CLASSIC BURGUNDIAN CHICKEN STEW

1 tbsp.	olive oil	15 mL
1 tbsp.	butter	15 mL
2	whole chicken breasts, boneless, skinless, cut into 1" (2.5 cm) square pieces	2
4 slices	bacon, chopped (optional)	4 slices
1	onion, coarsely chopped	1
½	rutabaga OR turnip, diced	½
2	carrots, diced	2
1 cup	chicken stock	250 mL
½ tsp.	salt	2 mL
¼ tsp.	pepper	1 mL
1 tsp.	crushed dried thyme	5 mL
1	bay leaf	1
¾ cup	dry red wine	175 mL
8	mushrooms, quartered	8

- In a heavy-bottomed Dutch oven, heat oil and butter. Add chicken pieces and brown. If using bacon, remove chicken from pan; sauté bacon until crisp, drain off most of fat. Return chicken to pan.
- Add onion, rutabaga, carrot, stock, salt, pepper, thyme and bay leaf. Cover; reduce heat to a simmer. Cook for 30-45 minutes, or until vegetables are just tender.
- Add the wine and mushrooms. Bring to a boil, then reduce heat; cover and simmer for an additional 15-20 minutes.
- Remove bay leaf. Serve hot.

VARIATIONS Substitute chicken thighs for the breasts; add 2 crushed garlic cloves. For a festive occasion, flame browned chicken breasts with about ¼ cup (60 mL) warmed brandy or Calvados.

YIELD *5 – 6 SERVINGS*

MEDITERRANEAN APRICOT & OLIVE CHICKEN

A FLAVORFUL MAKE-AHEAD ONE-DISH MEAL – PERFECT ANY TIME –
FROM ENTERTAINING TO PICNICS

4 lbs.	boneless chicken breasts & thighs	2 kg
8-10	garlic cloves, crushed	8-10
¼ cup	dried oregano OR Italian Seasoning	60 mL
½-1 tsp.	red pepper flakes	2-5 mL
	salt & pepper to taste	
½ cup	red wine vinegar	125 mL
½ cup	olive oil	125 mL
½ cup-1 cup	EACH dried apricots & pitted prunes	125-250 mL
½ cup	EACH pitted Spanish OR Greek black olives & green olives	125 mL
4	bay leaves	4
¼-½ cup	brown sugar	60-125 mL
1 cup	white wine	250 mL
¼ cup	chopped parsley for garnish	60 mL

- In a large shallow baking pan, combine chicken and all remaining ingredients, except parsley. Chicken should be in 1 or 2 layers.
- Cover with plastic wrap and marinate in the refrigerator overnight.
- Uncover and bake at 350°F (180°C) for 1-1½ hours, spooning marinade over chicken several times.
- Serve hot or at room temperature. Sprinkle each serving with chopped parsley. Serve with basmati or wild rice.

YIELD   8 – 10 SERVINGS

See photograph opposite.

MAIN COURSE – CHICKEN

Mediterranean Apricot & Olive Chicken, page 120
Couscous Chickpea Salad, page 91

Chicken, Sausage & Shrimp Jambalaya

A sensational and versatile Creole classic

3 tbsp.	vegetable OR olive oil	45 mL
2 lbs.	boneless chicken thighs or breasts	1 kg
2	celery stalks, chopped	2
1	medium onion, chopped	1
1	green OR red pepper, chopped	1
2-3	garlic cloves, minced	2-3

1 lb.	cooked smoked sausage – andouille
	    OR hot or mild Italian OR kielbasa,
	    cut into ½" (1.3 cm) slices
		500 g

2-3 tsp.	Cajun OR Creole seasoning	10-15 mL
2	bay leaves	2
28 oz.	can stewed tomatoes	796 mL
1	lemon	1
1 lb.	cooked, peeled, deveined shrimp salt & pepper to taste	500 g

- In a large skillet, heat oil and sauté chicken in batches until browned, set aside. Add celery, onion, pepper and garlic and sauté until tender, about 5 minutes.
- Reduce heat to a simmer. Add sausage, cajun seasoning, bay leaf, stewed tomatoes and chicken.
- Slice the lemon; cut slices into quarters. Add to tomato mixture. Simmer for 30 minutes, or until thickened.
- Add shrimp; simmer for about 5 minutes, or until heated through.
- Adjust flavoring with salt and pepper. Serve with cooked rice.

VARIATIONS   2 cups (500 mL) long-grain rice may be stirred into sautéed vegetable mixture. Add 4 cups (1 L) chicken stock with stewed tomatoes.

NOTE   For **Cajun** or **Creole Seasoning**, substitute 2 tsp. (10 mL) chili powder and ½ tsp. (2 mL) EACH cayenne pepper, dried thyme and oregano.

YIELD   **8 SERVINGS**

Greek Lemon Chicken with Potatoes

VERY POPULAR AND VERY GOOD

1 lb.	boneless, skinless, chicken thighs OR breasts	500 g
6	potatoes, peeled, sliced French-fry style	6
10	garlic cloves, peeled	10
2	lemons, juice of	2
½ cup	olive oil	125 mL
¼ cup	chicken stock, white wine OR water	60 mL
	salt, pepper & dried oregano to taste	

- In a lightly greased shallow baking pan, place chicken thighs in a single layer. Scatter potatoes around chicken. Scatter garlic cloves over.
- Combine lemon juice, olive oil and stock. Pour over chicken and potatoes.
- Sprinkle with salt and pepper to taste. Sprinkle with generous amounts of oregano, about 2 tsp. (10 mL).
- Bake, uncovered, at 350°F (180°C) for 30 minutes. Turn chicken and potatoes. If desired, sprinkle with additional oregano. Bake an additional 30 minutes, or until chicken is lightly browned and potatoes are soft when pricked.

VARIATIONS Add 2 cups (500 mL) sliced mushrooms. Capers are also a delicious addition – 2-3 tbsp. (30-45 mL).

YIELD **4 SERVINGS**

 Potatoes with low moisture content are best for baking, mashing and frying. These include russet, Idaho and long white potatoes. Boiling potatoes include round red and round white varieties, plus Yukon gold. They have a waxy texture that has less starch and more moisture than the baking potatoes. They are also good for roasting and frying. New potatoes of any variety are ideal for potato salad, boiling or pan-roasting.

CURRIED CHICKEN THIGHS

A WONDERFUL BASIC OR FESTIVE DISH – SERVE AS IS OR DRESS IT UP

1 tbsp.	EACH vegetable oil & butter	15 mL
2 lbs.	boneless, skinless chicken thighs	1 kg
3	onions, halved, sliced	3
3	garlic cloves, sliced	3
1½ cups	chicken stock	375 mL
1 tsp.-1 tbsp.	curry powder, or more, to taste	5-15 mL
¼ tsp.	ground ginger	1 mL
¼-½ tsp.	ground cumin	1-2 mL
½ tsp.	salt	2 mL
¼ tsp.	freshly grated pepper	1 mL
2 tbsp.	all-purpose flour	30 mL
½ cup	cereal OR half & half cream OR coconut milk	125 mL
1 cup	frozen peas (optional)	250 mL
1 cup	grape tomatoes	250 mL

- In a large skillet, heat oil and butter. Add chicken; sauté until browned on both sides. Add onions and garlic; sauté until onions are translucent.
- Add chicken stock and spices. Simmer gently until chicken is tender, about 20 minutes.
- Bring sauce to a boil; sprinkle with flour; add cream. Stir until thickened.
- Just prior to serving, stir in peas, if using, then add tomatoes; cook for only a minute.
- Serve hot, over steamed basmati rice, with mango chutney and, if you wish, shredded coconut, chopped toasted peanuts and sliced bananas.

VARIATIONS These are endless – try curry paste – vindaloo, masala, tikka, madras or tandoori; add a dash of cinnamon to the sauce; 1 tbsp. (15 mL) of tomato paste and ½ cup (125 mL) of mango chutney, applesauce or chopped apple are also good. Potatoes are delicious in curries. With the stock, add 2 cups (500 mL) of sliced or diced potato if you wish. A slivered red or yellow pepper and/or ½ cup (125 mL) chopped dried apricots are delicious additions.

YIELD ***6 – 8 SERVINGS***

GARLICKY STICKY CHICKEN THIGHS/WINGS

THE SAUCE CARAMELIZES AS THE CHICKEN BAKES

10-15	chicken thighs, skinned	10-15
	OR	
20-30	chicken wings, tips removed, wings split in 2 at the joint	20-30

GARLICKY SOY SAUCE:

¾ cup	soy sauce	175 mL
¼ cup	apple cider vinegar	60 mL
3	garlic cloves, minced	3
1	large onion, finely chopped	1
2 tbsp.	brown sugar	30 mL
2 tbsp.	ketchup	30 mL
2 tsp.	prepared mustard	10 mL
1 tsp.	ground ginger	5 mL
¼ tsp.	pepper	1 mL

- In a shallow roasting pan, place chicken pieces in a single layer.
- Combine sauce ingredients; pour over chicken.
- Bake at 350°F (180°C) for 40 minutes (wings) to 1 hour (thighs), turning chicken pieces every 10 to 15 minutes to distribute sauce.
- Serve hot or chill and serve cold.

YIELD   *8 SERVINGS*

CRISPY OVEN CHICKEN

LOWER FAT AND HIGH FLAVOR – A SURE WINNER

CRISPY COATING MIX:

2 cups	fine bread crumbs	500 mL
1 cup	all-purpose flour	250 mL
½ cup	dry chicken soup base	125 mL
¼ cup	paprika	60 mL
2 tbsp.	granulated garlic	30 mL
2 tbsp.	seasoning salt	30 mL
1 tbsp.	freshly ground pepper	15 mL
2 tsp.	poultry seasoning	10 mL
1 tsp.	ground ginger	5 mL
1 tsp.	ground nutmeg	5 mL
½ cup	vegetable oil	125 mL
2-3 lbs.	chicken pieces	1-1.5 kg

- In a large bowl, combine all coating ingredients, except vegetable oil. Pour vegetable oil over; mix well.
- Rinse chicken pieces in cold water; drain off excess moisture.
- Dip each piece into coating mix. Lay coated chicken pieces on an ungreased baking sheet.
- Bake at 350°F (180°C) for 25 minutes. Turn chicken pieces over. Bake for 20 minutes, or until chicken is thoroughly cooked.

YIELD   *4 – 6 SERVINGS; 4 CUPS (4 L) OF COATING MIX*
(freeze any remaining coating mix for future use)

CHICKEN CACCIATORE

HUNTER'S-STYLE CHICKEN – EVERY ITALIAN FAMILY HAS A FAVORITE RECIPE

½ cup	flour	125 mL
1 tsp.	salt	5 mL
¼ tsp.	pepper	1 mL
10	chicken thighs, skinned	10
2 tbsp.	butter	30 mL
2 tbsp.	olive OR vegetable oil	30 mL
2	garlic cloves, minced	2
1	large onion, sliced	1
½	green pepper, chopped	½
28 oz.	can Italian-style tomatoes	796 mL
1 tbsp.	dried parsley	15 mL
1 tsp.	dried oregano	5 mL
¼ tsp.	ground thyme	1 mL
2 cups	sliced mushrooms OR 10 oz. (284 mL) can mushroom stems & pieces, drained	500 mL
	salt & pepper to taste	

- In a plastic bag, combine flour, salt and pepper. Add chicken; shake bag to coat chicken pieces.
- In a large skillet, heat butter and oil. Add garlic and sauté briefly.
- Add chicken pieces to pan; brown on all sides.
- Add onion, pepper, tomatoes, parsley, oregano and thyme. Cover tightly; reduce heat to simmer. Cook for 30 minutes, stirring occasionally.
- Add mushrooms, salt and pepper. Continue to simmer for an additional 10 minutes, or until chicken is tender. Serve over rice, noodles or polenta.

VARIATION   Substitute 1½ tsp. (7 mL) EACH chopped fresh rosemary and sage, or ½ tsp. (2 mL) dried, for the parsley, oregano and thyme. Add ½ cup (125 mL) pitted, sliced Italian black olives.

YIELD   **6 – 8 SERVINGS**

CRANBERRY SAUSAGE DRESSING

A FESTIVE DRESSING WITH TURKEY OR CHICKEN

1 tbsp.	butter	15 mL
1	medium onion, chopped	1
2	celery stalks, chopped	2
13 oz.	pork sausage meat	370 g
2 cups	coarse bread crumbs	500 mL
1 tsp.	salt	5 mL
½ tsp.	pepper	2 mL
1 tbsp.	crushed dried sage	15 mL
1 tsp.	poultry seasoning	5 mL
¾ cup	whole-berry cranberry sauce	175 mL
1	egg	1
1 cup	water	250 mL

- In a large skillet, melt butter and sauté onion and celery just until tender. Add sausage meat and cook until no longer pink. Remove from heat.
- Stir in remaining ingredients. Spoon dressing into a lightly greased 6-cup (1.5 L) casserole.
- Bake at 350°F (180°C) for 30 minutes. Serve warm.

YIELD   *8 – 10 SERVINGS*

SUCCULENT ROAST BEEF

LOW HEAT FOR TENDER AND JUICY; HIGH HEAT FOR CRISP CRUST AND
RICH FLAVOR – THREE METHODS – YOUR CHOICE

3	large onions, thinly sliced	3
1 tbsp.	vegetable oil	15 mL
2-3	garlic cloves, crushed	2-3
	salt & pepper to taste	
1 tsp.	dried thyme	5 mL
4-6 lb.	boneless prime rib roast OR sirloin tip, rump, inside round or outside round roast	2-3 kg
1-2 cups	beef stock	250-500 mL
¼ cup	red wine	60 mL
1-2 tbsp.	Worcestershire sauce OR balsamic vinegar (optional)	15-30 mL
2-3 tbsp.	flour	30-45 mL
½ cup	water	125 mL

- In a roasting pan, combine onions and oil. Roast at 500°F (260°C) for 10 minutes.
- Combine garlic, salt, pepper and thyme. Rub over roast; place roast, fat side up, on top of onions. Insert meat thermometer.
- Reduce heat to 325°F (160°C). Roast, uncovered, for:
  - 20 minutes per pound (500 g) for rare (135°F/57°C)
  - 25 minutes per pound (500 g) for medium (155°F/68°C)
  - 30 minutes per pound (500 g) for well done (165°F/72°C)
- Remove roast to platter; cover with foil, shiny side in. Let rest for 15 minutes before carving. Roast temperature will rise 5°F (3°C),
- Pour off fat from roasting pan. Place pan over medium heat. Stir in stock, wine and Worcestershire sauce, if using. Bring to a boil, stirring occasionally.
- Shake flour with water; stir into gravy, cooking until thickened. Adjust seasoning, if needed, with additional thyme, salt and pepper.

Succulent Roast Beef

(Continued)

LOW-HEAT VARIATION   Preheat oven to 450°F (230°C) with oven rack one-third up from bottom. Cook roast for 10 minutes, then reduce heat to 250°F (120°C) and cook for 15 minutes per pound for rare to 30 minutes per pound for medium. Check with oven thermometer as above. Roast temperature will rise 5°F (3°C) while resting.

HIGH-HEAT VARIATION   Preheat oven to 425°F (220°C) with oven rack in center of oven. Do NOT reduce heat. Cook for 15 minutes per pound for rare to 20 minutes per pound for medium. Check with oven thermometer as above. Roast temperature will rise 10°F (6°C) while resting.

SEASONING VARIATIONS   *Coffee Rub* –1 tbsp. (15 mL) EACH demerara sugar, fine ground coffee or espresso, plus 1 tsp. (5 mL) EACH salt and pepper.

Sherry-Soy Glaze – ¼ cup (60 mL) EACH sherry, soy sauce, plus 1 tbsp. (15 mL) dry mustard. Baste roast during cooking.

Lime-Soy Glaze – 3 tbsp. (45 mL) EACH soy sauce, honey, plus 6 tbsp. (90 mL) fresh lime juice, 1½ tsp. (7 mL) cumin, ¾ tsp. (4 mL) Tabasco. Baste roast during cooking.

YIELD   *8 – 12 SERVINGS*

CLASSIC SAUERBRATEN

GERMAN CANADIAN COMFORT FOOD

6 lb.	sirloin tip roast	3 kg
2	onions, thinly sliced	2
1½ cups	red wine	325 mL
1½ cups	red wine vinegar	325 mL
8-10	juniper berries OR 1½ oz. (45 mL) gin	8-10
2	bay leaves	2
1 tsp.	black peppercorns	5 mL
3	whole cloves	3
2 tbsp.	salt	30 mL
¼ cup	vegetable oil	60 mL
5 tbsp.	flour	75 mL
4 tbsp.	butter	60 mL
1 tbsp.	sugar	15 mL
¼ tsp.	ground ginger	1 mL
¾ cup	crushed gingersnaps	175 mL

- Place roast and onions in a large sealable plastic bag. Combine wine, vinegar and seasonings; pour over roast in bag. Refrigerate for 3 days, turning roast occasionally.
- Remove roast from marinade; pat dry with paper towels.
- In a large Dutch oven, heat oil and brown roast over high heat. Sprinkle with 1 tbsp. (15 mL) flour.
- Strain marinade and add to pot. Cover roast; lower heat and simmer for 4-5 hours, until very tender.
- Remove meat and keep warm. Pour off stock and set aside. Melt remaining butter in pot; stir in remaining flour, sugar and ginger until smooth. Stir in stock; cook until thickened. Add gingersnaps, stirring until dissolved. Return meat to pot and cook 30-40 minutes longer.
- Serve over buttered egg noodles with sautéed red cabbage, see page 54 in *Grandma's Touch*.

VARIATION   Stir 1 cup (250 mL) sour cream into the sauce.

YIELD   *12 – 14 SERVINGS*

BEEF 'N' BROCCOLI STIR-FRY

AN ASIAN CLASSIC

1 tbsp.	soy sauce	15 mL
1 tbsp.	cornstarch	15 mL
⅛ tsp.	pepper	0.5 mL
1 lb.	sirloin tip OR flank steak, thinly sliced	450 g
1 lb.	broccoli	450 g
1 tbsp.	vegetable oil	15 mL
½ tsp.	salt	2 mL
¼ cup	water	60 mL
1 tbsp.	vegetable oil	15 mL
3	garlic cloves, minced	3

- In a shallow dish, combine soy sauce, cornstarch and pepper. Add beef and mix to coat. Let marinate for 20 minutes.
- Cut broccoli head into florets. Cut the broccoli stalks diagonally into bite-sized slices.
- In a wok, over high heat, heat 1 tbsp. (15 mL) oil. Add broccoli, salt and water. Stir, then cover. Cook for 3 minutes, or until the steam escapes. Transfer broccoli to a warm dish.
- In the wok, heat remaining 1 tbsp. (15 mL) oil. Add garlic cloves; brown for a minute. Add marinated beef; stir-fry until browned. Return broccoli to wok. Toss with beef. Serve immediately.

VARIATIONS With the broccoli, add 1 medium onion, chopped, and with the garlic, add 1 red pepper, slivered.

YIELD *4 – 6 SERVINGS*

MOUSSAKA

ORIGINALLY GREEK – NOW A FAVORITE THROUGHOUT THE MIDDLE EAST
AND NORTH AMERICA

1	large eggplant	1
	salt	
	oil	

MEAT SAUCE:

2 tbsp.	olive oil	30 mL
1	large onion, chopped	1
2-3	garlic cloves, crushed	2-3
1½ lbs.	lean ground beef OR lamb	680 g
2	Roma tomatoes, chopped	2
2 tbsp.	tomato paste	30 mL
½ cup	white OR red wine	125 mL
¼ cup	chopped fresh parsley OR 1 tbsp. (15 mL) dried	60 mL
1 tsp.	sugar	5 mL
¼ tsp.	EACH cinnamon & nutmeg	1 mL
	salt & pepper to taste	
½ tsp.	dried crushed oregano	2 mL

BÉCHAMEL SAUCE:

¼ cup	butter	60 mL
¼ cup	all-purpose flour	60 mL
2 cups	milk	500 mL
¼ tsp.	nutmeg	1 mL
2 tbsp.	grated Parmesan cheese	30 mL
	salt & pepper to taste	
1	egg, lightly beaten	1

TOPPING:

| ⅓ cup | dry bread crumbs | 75 mL |
| ⅓ cup | grated Parmesan cheese | 75 mL |

MOUSSAKA

(CONTINUED)

- Cut eggplant into ¼" (1 cm) slices; place on paper towels. Sprinkle slices with salt; let drain for at least an hour.
- Pat eggplant dry with paper towels. In a skillet, heat oil, pan-fry eggplant slices. Set aside.
- **For meat sauce**, in a large skillet, heat oil; sauté onion and garlic. Add meat; sauté until meat is no longer pink. Add remaining sauce ingredients; simmer gently for 20 minutes.
- **For Béchamel sauce**, in a heavy-bottomed saucepan, over medium heat, melt butter. Stir in flour and cook gently. Add milk while continuing to cook and stir. Bring to a boil, cook for 1 minute; remove from heat. Add nutmeg, Parmesan, salt and pepper. Stir until cheese is melted and sauce is smooth. Stir some of the hot sauce into the egg; return to saucepan.
- In a small bowl, combine topping ingredients.
- To assemble, lightly grease a 9 x 13" (23 x 33 cm) baking dish. Arrange layers of ½ of the eggplant slices, meat sauce, the other half of the eggplant and the Béchamel sauce. Sprinkle with crumb mixture.
- Bake at 350°F (180°C) for 1 hour. Remove from oven. Let sit for 15-20 minutes to cool slightly; cut into squares.

VARIATIONS   Substitute grated Greek kefalotiri cheese for the Parmesan.

For a *Vegetarian Moussaka*, omit the ground meat and add 2 cups (500 mL) EACH, thinly sliced zucchini, potatoes, mushrooms. Sauté with onion and garlic and proceed as above.

YIELD   *6 – 8 SERVINGS*

PASTITSIO

THIS POPULAR LAYERED GREEK PASTA COMBINES TWO FAVORITES –
PASTA WITH MEAT SAUCE AND MACARONI AND CHEESE

TOMATO MEAT SAUCE:

1 tbsp.	olive oil	15 mL
1	onion, chopped	1
2-3	garlic cloves, minced	2-3
1½ lbs.	lean ground beef OR lamb	680 g
19 oz.	can plum tomatoes	540 mL
7.5 oz.	can tomato sauce	213 mL
½ cup	red wine (optional)	125 mL
1 tsp.	dried crushed oregano	5 mL
¼ tsp.	EACH cinnamon & nutmeg	1 mL
	salt & pepper to taste	

PASTA LAYER:

½ cup	fine bread crumbs	125 mL
2 cups	uncooked macaroni	500 mL
2 tbsp.	butter	30 mL
2	eggs, lightly beaten	2

BÉCHAMEL SAUCE:

3 tbsp.	butter	45 mL
¼ cup	all-purpose flour	60 mL
2 cups	milk	500 mL
⅓ cup	grated Parmesan cheese	75 mL
⅛ tsp.	nutmeg	0.5 mL
	pepper to taste	

- **For meat sauce**, in a large skillet, heat oil and cook onion and garlic. Add beef and brown. Add tomatoes, tomato sauce, wine and seasonings. Simmer for 30 minutes, or until liquid has been absorbed.
- Sprinkle bread crumbs into a buttered 9 x 13" (23 x 33 cm) baking pan. Cook macaroni according to package directions; drain. Add butter and eggs; mix well. Spread half of cooked macaroni over bread crumbs.

PASTITSIO

(CONTINUED)

- Layer meat sauce over macaroni. Add remaining half of macaroni.
- **For Béchamel sauce**, in a saucepan, over low heat, melt butter. Stir in flour. While stirring, slowly add milk. Cook until thickened. Add Parmesan cheese, nutmeg and pepper. Pour over macaroni.
- Bake at 350°F (180°C) for 1 hour, or until golden. Let stand for 15 minutes to cool slightly; cut into squares.

YIELD   *8 SERVINGS*

BLACK BEAN CHILI

BLACK OR TURTLE BEANS HAVE AN EARTHY SWEET FLAVOR

2 tbsp.	olive oil	30 mL
1	medium onion, chopped	1
2	garlic cloves, minced	2
2	stalks celery, chopped	2
1	green OR red pepper, diced	1
1 lb.	extra-lean ground beef	450 g
2 x 19 oz.	cans black turtle beans, drained	2 x 540 mL
28 oz.	can Italian-style peeled tomatoes	796 mL
1	jalapeño pepper, minced	1
1-3 tbsp.	chili powder, or more, to taste	15-45 mL
	salt & pepper to taste	

- In a Dutch oven, over medium-high heat, heat oil and sauté onion, garlic, celery, pepper and beef until beef is no longer pink.
- Add remaining ingredients, reduce heat; simmer for 1-2 hours.

YIELD   *6 – 8 SERVINGS*

BEEF STROGANOFF

RUSSIAN IN ORIGIN – CANADIAN BY ADOPTION

1 tbsp.	butter	15 mL
1 lb.	sirloin tip, beef tenderloin OR top loin steak	450 g
1	medium onion, chopped	1
10-12	mushrooms, sliced	10-12
1½ cups	beef stock	375 mL
3 tbsp.	tomato paste	45 mL
1 tsp.	Dijon mustard	5 mL
1 tbsp.	Worcestershire sauce (optional)	15 mL
¾ tsp.	Hungarian paprika	4 mL
1 tsp.	salt	5 mL
½ tsp.	pepper	2 mL
2	garlic cloves, minced	2
3 tbsp.	all-purpose flour	45 mL
1 cup	sour cream	250 mL
	chopped fresh parsley for garnish	

- Cut beef into ½ x 1½" (1.3 x 4 cm) strips.
- In a 10" (25 cm) skillet, over medium heat, melt butter and brown beef, stirring occasionally. Add onion and mushrooms; cook until onion is tender.
- Set aside ½ cup (125 mL) of the beef stock. To the other cup of stock, add tomato paste, mustard, Worcestershire sauce, paprika, salt, pepper and garlic; mix well. Pour over beef and vegetables. Bring to a boil; reduce heat and cover; simmer until beef is tender, about 20 minutes.
- To reserved beef stock, add flour; blend well. Stir gradually into beef mixture. Bring to a boil; stir for a couple of minutes before reducing heat to a simmer. Stir in sour cream.
- Serve over rice pilaf, spaetzle noodles, fettuccini or mashed potatoes, with Garlicky Cherry Tomatoes, page 98.

VARIATION   Add ¼ cup (60 mL) of sherry or dry red wine to the tomato paste mixture.

YIELD   *6 SERVINGS*

MAIN COURSE – PASTA

Pasta Puttanesca, page 152
Lebanese Bread Salad, page 90

TEX-MEX LASAGNE

AN ITALIAN FAVORITE WITH A SOUTHERN TWIST

1½ lbs.	extra-lean ground beef	680 g
1	medium onion, chopped	1
2	garlic cloves, minced	2
14 oz.	jar of enchilada sauce	398 mL
14 oz.	can diced tomatoes	398 mL
20	pitted, chopped ripe olives (optional)	20
1 tsp.	seasoned salt	5 mL
¼ tsp.	freshly ground pepper	1 mL
1 cup	fat-free cottage cheese	250 mL
1	egg	1
8 oz.	Jalapeño-flavored Monterey Jack cheese, thinly sliced	250 g
6	10" (25 cm) tortillas, flour or corn, quartered	6
1 cup	shredded Cheddar cheese	250 mL

- In a large skillet, sauté beef, onions and garlic. Add sauce, tomatoes, olives, salt and pepper. Bring to a boil, then reduce heat; simmer, uncovered, for 20-30 minutes.
- In a small bowl, combine cottage cheese and egg.
- Lightly grease a 9 x 13 x 2" (23 x 33 x 5 cm) baking dish.
- Layer the ingredients in the pan as follows: ⅓ meat sauce, ½ Monterey Jack cheese, ½ cottage cheese and ½ tortillas. Repeat these layers. Spread remaining ⅓ of meat sauce on top. Sprinkle with Cheddar cheese.
- Bake, covered, at 350°F (180°C) for 20 minutes. Uncover and bake for 15 minutes more, or until thoroughly heated and cheese is melted.
- Let stand for 10 minutes to cool slightly; cut into squares.

YIELD   8 SERVINGS

MEXICALI BEEF PIE

A CRUSTY GOLDEN TOPPING AND ZESTY FILLING

1 tbsp.	olive oil	15 mL
1 lb.	lean ground beef	450 g
1	medium onion, finely chopped	1
1	garlic clove, minced	1
1 tbsp.	taco seasoning, see below	15 mL
4	pickled hot cherry OR jalapeño peppers, chopped	4
1¼ cups	flour	300 mL
½ tsp.	salt	2 mL
2 tsp.	baking powder	10 mL
2 tbsp.	butter OR margarine	30 mL
1½ cups	skim milk	375 mL
3	eggs	3
3 oz.	Monterey Jack OR Cheddar cheese, grated	85 g

- In a skillet, over medium-high heat, heat oil and brown beef. Add onion and garlic; cook until onions are tender. Remove from heat.
- Stir in taco seasoning and peppers. Transfer meat mixture to a lightly greased 2½-quart (2.5 L) or larger ovenproof casserole.
- In a medium bowl, combine flour, salt and baking powder. With a pastry blender cut in butter until the mixture resembles coarse meal. Add milk and eggs. Using a wire whisk, beat until smooth. Pour over meat mixture in casserole.
- Bake at 350°F (180°C) for 30 to 35 minutes, or until topping is puffed and lightly browned. Sprinkle with cheese. Return to oven for an additional 5 minutes, or until cheese is melted.

YIELD   4 – 6 SERVINGS

 To make your own *Taco Seasoning*, combine 1 part black pepper, 1 part garlic powder, 2 parts ground cumin, 2 parts onion powder, 2 parts salt, 4 parts dried oregano, 4 parts chili powder.

OSSO BUCO (BRAISED VEAL SHANKS)

SLOW COOKING ALLOWS THE FLAVORS TO DEEPEN AND MELLOW

3½ lbs.	veal shanks, 1-1½" (2.5-4 cm) thick	1.6 kg
1 cup	all-purpose flour	250 mL
1 tsp.	salt	5 mL
½ tsp.	pepper	2 mL
2 tbsp.	butter	30 mL
1 tbsp.	olive oil	15 mL
1	onion, coarsely chopped	1
4	carrots, peeled, chopped	4
3	celery stalks, chopped	3
4	garlic cloves, finely minced	4
1 cup	EACH white wine & chicken stock	250 mL
1 tsp.	dried basil	5 mL
3	bay leaves	3
¼ tsp.	dried thyme	1 mL
3	Roma tomatoes, finely chopped	3

GREMOLATA:

4	garlic cloves, minced	4
1 cup	chopped fresh parsley	250 mL
1 tbsp.	freshly grated lemon zest	15 mL

- With cooking string, tie veal shanks around the circumference and around the top and bottom to keep the marrow in place.
- Combine flour, salt and pepper. Dredge veal shanks in flour mixture.
- In a skillet, heat butter and oil; brown shanks on both sides. Transfer shanks to a large shallow baking dish with a tight-fitting lid.
- Add onion, carrots, celery and garlic to skillet; cook for 1-2 minutes. Spoon vegetables over shanks in baking dish.
- To skillet, add wine, stock, basil, bay leaves and thyme. Stir to deglaze skillet. Bring to a boil. Pour over shanks. Spoon tomatoes on top.
- Cover pan and place in a 300°F (150°C) oven. Braise for 3-4 hours.
- For gremolata, combine garlic, parsley and lemon zest.
- Serve veal shanks and vegetables topped with gremolata.

YIELD   ***6 SERVINGS***

VEAL PARMIGIANA

TENDER CUTLETS IN A GOLDEN PARMESAN CRUST – SUBLIME!

½ cup	all-purpose flour	125 mL
½ tsp.	salt	2 mL
¼ tsp.	pepper	1 mL
2	eggs	2
1 tbsp.	milk	15 mL
¾ cup	fine bread crumbs	175 mL
⅓ cup	grated Parmesan cheese	75 mL
6	veal cutlets	6
2 tbsp.	vegetable oil	30 mL
1 tbsp.	Italian seasoning	15 mL
7½ oz.	can tomato sauce	213 mL
6	slices Mozzarella cheese	6
6 tbsp.	grated Parmesan cheese	90 mL

- Set out 3 shallow dishes. In the first, combine flour, salt and pepper.
- Whisk eggs with milk; place in second dish.
- Combine bread crumbs and Parmesan cheese in the third dish.
- Dip each cutlet in flour; shake off excess. Dip in egg wash to coat completely. Dip in crumb mixture, pressing gently to coat cutlet completely.
- In a large skillet, heat oil. Pan-fry cutlets on both sides until golden brown. Transfer cutlets to a shallow baking pan.
- Sprinkle cutlets with Italian seasoning, then spoon tomato sauce over.
- Top each cutlet with a slice of Mozzarella; sprinkle each with 1 tbsp. (15 mL) of Parmesan.
- Bake at 350°F (180°C) for 15 minutes, or until cheese is melted. Serve immediately.

YIELD   4 – 6 SERVINGS

PORK SATAY

GREAT AS A MAIN COURSE OVER RICE OR AS AN APPETIZER

	wooden skewers, soaked in water	
1½ lbs.	pork tenderloin, 1" (2.5 cm) cubed	680 g

LEMON GARLIC MARINADE:

2 tbsp.	butter	30 mL
1	lemon, juice & grated zest	1
½ tsp.	hot pepper sauce	2 mL
½	onion, finely chopped	½
1 tbsp.	brown sugar	15 mL
1 tsp.	ground coriander	5 mL
½ tsp.	ground cumin	2 mL
1 tbsp.	finely chopped fresh ginger	15 mL
2	garlic cloves, crushed	2
¾ cup	soy sauce	175 mL
½ tsp.	freshly grated pepper	2 mL

- Prepare skewers.
- Place cubed pork into a heavy-duty sealable plastic bag.
- In a small saucepan, over medium heat, melt butter. Add remaining ingredients; bring to a boil. Reduce heat; simmer for about 5 minutes. Pour marinade over meat; seal bag and refrigerate overnight, turning meat periodically to distribute marinade.
- When ready to cook, remove pork cubes from marinade and thread onto wooden skewers. Grill on a preheated barbecue for 12-15 minutes.

YIELD   6 SERVINGS

See photograph on page 85.

Pork Chops à la Orange

MARMALADE AND APPLE CIDER VINEGAR MAKE A TANGY SAUCE

6	boneless pork loin chops	6
1 tbsp.	vegetable oil	15 mL
	salt & pepper to taste	
¾ cup	unsweetened orange juice	175 mL
2 tbsp.	brown sugar	30 mL
2 tbsp.	orange marmalade	30 mL
1 tbsp.	apple cider vinegar	15 mL
1 tbsp.	cornstarch	15 mL
2 tbsp.	cold water	30 mL

- In a large skillet, over medium-high heat, heat oil and brown pork chops. Sprinkle with salt and pepper.
- Combine orange juice, sugar, marmalade and vinegar. Pour over pork chops. Simmer for 15 minutes. Remove chops and keep warm.
- Combine cornstarch and cold water. Add to orange juice mixture; bring to a boil until thickened. Serve sauce over pork chops and steamed rice.

YIELD   4 SERVINGS

Pork Loin Roast with Peach Sauce

GARNISH WITH FRESH PEACH SLICES IN SEASON

¼ cup	EACH sherry & soy sauce	60 mL
2-3 lb.	boneless pork loin roast	1-1.5 kg
1 cup	canned sliced peaches, drained	250 mL
¼ cup	brown sugar	60 mL
¼ cup	ketchup	60 mL
¼ cup	white vinegar	60 mL
1 tbsp.	soy sauce	15 mL
2	garlic cloves	2
1 tsp.	ground ginger	5 mL

PORK LOIN ROAST WITH PEACH SAUCE
(CONTINUED)

- A day before serving, combine sherry and soy sauce. Place in a sealable plastic bag with the roast. Marinate overnight in refrigerator; turn occasionally to coat roast.
- In a food processor, combine the remaining ingredients.
- Roast pork loin at 325°F (160°C) for 1½-2 hours. During the last half hour of roasting, baste 3-4 times with the peach sauce.

VARIATION   Substitute mangoes or fresh nectarines for peaches.

YIELD   **6 – 8 SERVINGS**

ORANGE-MARINATED BARBECUED PORK
ORANGE JUICE AND HERBS – A SUPERB MARINADE

12 oz.	can frozen orange juice concentrate, thawed	340 g
2 cups	water	500 mL
½ cup	packed brown sugar	125 mL
1 tsp.	salt	5 mL
1 tsp.	EACH dried marjoram & rosemary	5 mL
½ tsp.	freshly ground coarse pepper	2 mL
2-3 lb.	boneless pork loin roast	1-1.5 kg

- Combine all marinade ingredients. Place in a sealable plastic bag with the roast. Marinate roast overnight in the refrigerator. Remove pork and reserve marinade.
- Cook pork on rotisserie according to manufacturer's directions. Brush with reserved sauce 2-3 times during last half hour of cooking.

YIELD   **6 – 8 SERVINGS**

POLISH HUNTER'S STEW (BIGOS)

ONE OF THE GREAT PEASANT DISHES OF THE WORLD

1 oz.	dried Polish (*Boletus*) OR porcini mushrooms	30 g
4 cups	sauerkraut, rinsed, drained	1 L
1½ lbs.	pork back ribs	680 g
2	bay leaves	2
20	black peppercorns	20
2	whole allspice berries	2
2-3	garlic cloves, minced	2-3
6 cups	beef stock	1.5 L
½	medium cabbage, finely chopped	½
	Maggi seasoning to taste	
10 oz.	Polish smoked sausage (kielbasa), cubed	300 g
8 oz.	bacon	225 g
1 tbsp.	butter	15 mL
1	medium onion, chopped	1
	salt & pepper to taste	

- Soak dried mushrooms in boiling water for at least 30 minutes; drain.
- In a large stockpot, combine sauerkraut, ribs, bay leaves, peppercorns, allspice berries, garlic and stock. Bring to a boil; reduce heat, cover and simmer for 2 hours, or until ribs are tender. Remove ribs; cool.
- Add cabbage to sauerkraut mixture; simmer until cabbage is tender.
- Remove meat from ribs; cut into ¼" (1 cm) cubes.
- In a skillet, fry bacon until crisp; drain on paper toweling; crumble.
- Melt butter in skillet; sauté onion until translucent.
- Add pork rib meat, sausage, bacon, mushrooms, onion, salt and pepper to sauerkraut mixture. Cover; simmer until thoroughly heated, about 30-40 minutes. Discard bay leaves. Serve hot with sour cream, boiled potatoes, rye bread and beer. This is even better the next day.

VARIATIONS	Replace 2 cups (500 mL) of beef stock with dry white or red wine OR use 1 cup (250 mL) EACH white wine and apple cider. Add 8 juniper berries, crushed, or 2 tbsp. (30 mL) gin.
NOTE	Maggi is a basic in European kitchens. Fresh maggi, also known as lovage or sea parsley, has a strong celery flavor and fragrance.
YIELD	***10 SERVINGS***

BEAN SAUSAGE HOT POT

A HEARTY DISH WITH AN EARTHY, ZESTY FLAVOR

2 cups	Six Bean Mix, see below	500 mL
	water	
2 x 5½ oz.	cans of tomato paste	2 x 156 mL
1 lb.	fresh chorizo sausage, sliced	450 g
1 tbsp.	olive oil	15 mL
1	onion, chopped	1
2	celery stalks, chopped	2
2	garlic cloves, minced	2
½ tsp.	ground cumin	2 mL
1 tsp.	ground oregano	5 mL
½ tsp.	freshly ground pepper	2 mL

- Place beans in a pot and cover liberally with water. Let soak overnight.
- Drain beans, then add 6 cups (1.5 L) of water. Bring to a boil; reduce heat, cover and cook for 1 hour, or until all beans are tender but firm.
- Add tomato paste and continue to simmer.
- Meanwhile, in a skillet, heat oil and sauté sausage slices. When thoroughly cooked, transfer sausage to the bean mixture. Drain off all but 1 tbsp. (15 mL) of fat.
- In the skillet, sauté onion and celery until tender. Add sautéed vegetables to bean mixture with the spices. Continue to simmer for 50-60 minutes to allow flavors to blend.

YIELD   8 SERVINGS

SIX BEAN MIX

1 cup	EACH dried white, red kidney, lima, black, yellow-eyed and Romano beans	250 mL

- Combine all beans. Store in a sealed container in a dry place until ready to use in soups, stews or other dishes.

Pasta Perogies

UKRAINIAN PEROGY FLAVOR WITHOUT THE FUSS

36	giant pasta shells	36
1 tbsp.	vegetable oil	15 mL
2 tbsp.	butter	30 mL
1	medium onion, chopped	1
6 slices	smoked maple ham	6 slices
4	medium potatoes, cooked, mashed	4
⅓ cup	sour cream	75 mL
1 cup	grated Cheddar cheese	250 mL
	sour cream	
	prosciutto	

- In a pasta pot, cook pasta in 3 quarts (3 L) of boiling water until just tender to bite, about 10-12 minutes. Drain; immerse pasta in cold water to which oil has been added. When cool, drain; shake gently to remove water from inside shells.
- Cut ham into ¼" (0.5 cm) pieces.
- In a large skillet, melt butter; sauté onion and ham until onion is translucent. Mix half of ham mixture into potatoes with the sour cream. Spoon potato mixture into cooked pasta shells.
- Arrange filled shells in a lightly greased shallow baking pan. Sprinkle remaining onion-ham mixture and cheese over shells. Cover.
- Bake at 350°F (180°C) for 20-25 minutes, or until thoroughly heated. If desired, serve with additional sour cream and prosciutto.

YIELD   8 SERVINGS

Proscuitto is an air-dried, salt-cured ham from Italy. Parma ham or prosciutto di Parma is the original. Delicious with melons and figs, it is available in many super-markets. If adding it to cooked dishes, add at the end, as it gets tough when overcooked.

Pasta Carbonara

THE HOT PASTA COOKS THE EGGS TO MAKE A DELECTABLE SAUCE

1 tbsp.	olive oil	15 mL
1 tbsp.	butter	15 mL
¼ lb.	prosciutto, panchetta OR lean bacon, thinly sliced	125 g
3	eggs, well beaten	3
½ cup	grated Parmesan cheese	125 mL
¼ cup	chopped fresh parsley	60 mL
½ tsp.	salt	2 mL
¼ tsp.	freshly ground pepper	1 mL
8 oz.	spaghetti	250 g
	grated Parmesan cheese	
	freshly ground pepper	
	chopped parsley	

- In a medium skillet, over medium heat, heat oil and butter. Add prosciutto; cook until browned but not crisp. Drain; set aside.
- In a small bowl, combine eggs, ½ cup (125 mL) Parmesan cheese, parsley, salt and pepper. Set aside.
- In a large pot of boiling water, cook spaghetti until tender but firm. Drain; return to hot pot. Return pot to turned off, but warm, burner. Quickly pour egg mixture over spaghetti, tossing with 2 forks.
- Add prosciutto; toss again.
- Serve immediately with additional Parmesan cheese, black pepper and parsley.

NOTE   Pancetta is a salt-cured Italian bacon. Also see proscuitto note on page 150.

YIELD   *4 SERVINGS*

PASTA PUTTANESCA

INTENSE FLAVORS AND A RACY HISTORY —
CREATED BY ITALIAN LADIES OF THE EVENING

1 tbsp.	olive oil	15 mL
2	garlic cloves, minced	2
¼-½ tsp.	red chili pepper flakes	1-2 mL
1	medium onion, chopped	1
4	plum tomatoes, chopped OR 19 oz. (540 mL) can plum tomatoes, drained, chopped	4
1 cup	tomato juice	250 mL
10	Kalamata OR Niçoise olives, pitted, sliced	10
2 tbsp.	drained capers	30 mL
4	anchovy fillets, coarsely chopped	
1 tbsp.	EACH chopped fresh basil & oregano OR 1 tsp. (5 mL) EACH dried	15 mL
¼ cup	chopped parsley	60 mL
	salt & pepper to taste	
8 oz.	uncooked capellini, fusilli, or linguine	250 g

- In a medium skillet, over medium heat, heat oil. Add garlic, pepper flakes and onion. Sauté until onions are soft. Add remaining ingredients, except pasta. Simmer for 10-15 minutes, or until tomatoes are tender and sauce has thickened slightly.
- Meanwhile, in a large pot, cook pasta in 3-quarts (3 L) of boiling water just until tender to bite. Drain.
- Serve pasta warm, topped with sauce.

VARIATION   Cooked shrimp, crab or canned tuna may be added to the sauce to heat through while sauce thickens. Dried, rehydrated, porcini or shitake mushrooms add interesting flavor.

YIELD   *4 SERVINGS*

See photograph on page 139.

DESSERTS

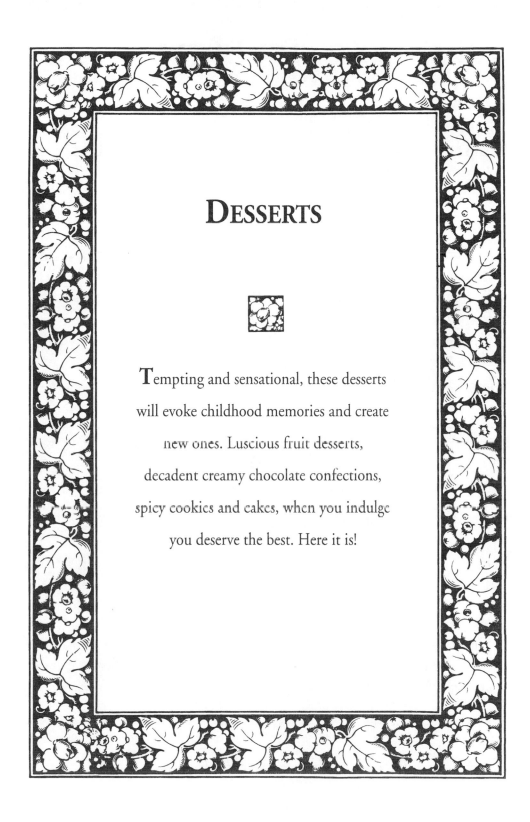

Tempting and sensational, these desserts will evoke childhood memories and create new ones. Luscious fruit desserts, decadent creamy chocolate confections, spicy cookies and cakes, when you indulge you deserve the best. Here it is!

CHOCOLATE FONDUE

A LEISURELY, SUMPTUOUS DESSERT – GRANDCHILDREN LOVE THIS

8 oz.	milk, semisweet or bittersweet chocolate	250 g
½ cup	half 'n' half (cereal) cream	125 mL
1-2 tbsp.	brandy or selected liqueur (optional)	15-30 mL
	variety of fresh fruit	
	pound cake, see page 182	

- In a heavy saucepan, over low heat, melt chocolate with cream, stirring until smooth. Remove from heat. If desired, add liqueur.
- Pour into a chocolate fondue pot set over a tea light. Surround with fresh fruit and with cake cut into bite-sized pieces.
- Using fondue forks, dip pieces of fresh fruit, dried apricots and cake into chocolate.

YIELD   *8 SERVINGS*

STRAWBERRY COULIS

FRESH FRUIT COULIS (KU:LIS) MAKE LOVELY SAUCES FOR CAKES AND ICE CREAM

1 lb.	fresh strawberries	500 g
1	lemon, juice of	1
¼ cup	sugar	60 mL
1 tbsp.	strawberry-flavored liqueur OR	15 mL
	Grand Marnier	

- Finely chop strawberries. Place in a bowl with lemon juice, sugar and liqueur. Purée until smooth. Strain to remove any seeds. Serve or cover and refrigerate for up to 3 days.

VARIATION   For **Fruit Coulis**, replace strawberries with raspberries, blueberries, kiwi, peaches OR mangoes. Taste the purée and adjust the sugar and lemon juice.

YIELD   *ABOUT 1 CUP (250 ML) OF COULIS*

STRAWBERRY MERINGUE HEARTS

PERFECT FOR YOUR VALENTINE, OR ANY SPECIAL OCCASION

3	egg whites	3
¼ tsp.	cream of tartar	1 mL
¾ cup	sugar	175 mL
1 lb.	fresh strawberries, sliced	500 g
	strawberry coulis, see page 154	
1 cup	whipping cream, whipped	250 mL

- Line a large cookie sheet with foil. Using a 4" (10 cm) heart-shaped cookie cutter or cardboard template as a guide, with a toothpick, carefully outline 6 heart shapes on foil.
- Preheat oven to 275°F (140°C).
- In small mixing bowl, with mixer at high speed, beat egg whites and cream of tartar until soft peaks form. Sprinkle in sugar, 2 tbsp. (30 mL) at a time, beating well after each addition. Sugar should be completely dissolved and egg whites should stand in stiff, glossy peaks.
- Spoon meringue into a large decorating bag with a medium star tip. Pipe meringue onto the heart shapes on the cookie sheet. Pipe remaining meringue in a decorative star border around heart shapes, forming "nests" about 1" (2.5 cm) high around edges.
- Bake meringues in preheated oven for 45 minutes. Turn oven off but leave meringues in oven for an additional hour to dry completely. DO NOT OPEN OVEN DOOR.
- Cool meringues on cookie sheet on a wire rack for 10 minutes. With a metal spatula, carefully loosen meringues and remove from foil to wire rack until completely cool. Once cooled, store meringues in a tightly covered container until ready to use.
- To serve, arrange meringues on individual serving plates. Fill "nests" with fresh strawberries, drizzle with strawberry coulis, place a dollop of whipped cream on top and drizzle with more coulis.

YIELD   6 SERVINGS

RASPBERRY WHITE CHOCOLATE TIRAMISU

A GRAND FINALE FOR A SPECIAL DINNER

2 x 15 oz.	pkgs. frozen raspberries in light syrup, thawed	2 x 425 g
2 tbsp.	raspberry liqueur	30 mL
2 tbsp.	cornstarch	30 mL
3	egg yolks	3
½ cup	sugar	125 mL
⅓ cup	raspberry liqueur	75 mL
2 cups	mascarpone cheese	500 mL
1 cup	whipping cream, whipped	250 mL
24	ladyfingers	24
4 oz.	white chocolate, shaved	115 g

- Strain raspberries and reserve juice. Set aside some whole raspberries.
- Combine 3 tbsp. juice with 2 tbsp. (30 mL) liqueur. Set aside.
- In a small bowl, mix cornstarch with 3 tbsp. (45 mL) juice. Heat remaining juice in a small saucepan. Add some hot juice to the cornstarch mixture, then pour cornstarch mixture into saucepan. Cook gently until thickened. Cool; stir in raspberries. Sauce should be of jam consistency.
- **For custard**, in the top of a double boiler, not over heat, whisk egg yolks with sugar until light. Whisk in ⅓ cup (75 mL) liqueur. Place over double boiler bottom and cook gently over simmering water, whisking constantly, until thick and creamy. Remove from heat and cool.
- In a large bowl, beat cheese until smooth. Add cooled custard. Gently fold in whipped cream.
- In a clear glass serving dish, layer ½ of lady fingers, cutting to fit if necessary. Brush ladyfingers with ½ of juice-liqueur mixture. Spread with ⅓ of custard, then ½ of raspberries and ⅓ of chocolate. Layer with other ½ of ladyfingers, brushed with juice-liqueur mixture, ⅓ of custard, remaining raspberries and ⅓ of chocolate. Top with remaining custard; then chocolate. Garnish with reserved raspberries.
- Cover with plastic wrap and refrigerate for a least 6 hours or overnight.

YIELD   8 SERVINGS

See photograph opposite.

DESSERTS

Raspberry White Chocolate Tiramisu, page 156

Coeur à la Crème

Easy but truly decadent!

Raspberry Sauce:

15 oz.	package frozen raspberries, thawed, drained	425 g
½ cup	red currant jelly, melted	125 mL
1 tbsp.	strawberry OR raspberry-flavored liqueur	15 mL
2 cups	whipping cream	500 mL
6 oz.	cream cheese	170 g
⅓ cup	icing (confectioner's) sugar	75 mL
1 tsp.	vanilla extract	5 mL
3 cups	fresh strawberries, hulled	750 mL

- **For sauce**, blend raspberries, jelly and liqueur. Press through a sieve to remove raspberry seeds. Refrigerate until ready to serve.
- Line a 3½-cup (875 mL) coeur à la crème mold (a heart-shaped metal or porcelain mold with holes in the bottom for drainage) with a piece of cheesecloth which has been rinsed in cold water and wrung out. Cheesecloth should be large enough to line the mold and cover the filling.
- **For filling**, in a large chilled bowl, beat whipping cream until it holds its shape but is not stiff.
- In a large bowl, beat cream cheese until light and fluffy. Gradually beat in sugar and vanilla. Gently fold in whipped cream. Spread mixture into cheesecloth-lined mold. Fold the cheesecloth over the filling. Place mold on a plate to catch the whey that drains off. Refrigerate until ready to serve.
- To serve, unmold the Coeur à la Crème onto a serving platter; surround with strawberries.
- Drizzle Raspberry Sauce over individual servings or pass the sauce in a pitcher.

YIELD   ***8 SERVINGS***

Jelly Roll with Strawberries and Cream

Vary the filling with seasonal fresh fruit

4	egg whites, room temperature	4
½ tsp.	cream of tartar	2 mL
½ cup	sugar	125 mL
4	egg yolks	4
½ cup	sugar	125 mL
¼ cup	water	60 mL
2 tsp.	vanilla extract	10 mL
1 cup	sifted cake flour	250 mL
¼ tsp.	salt	1 mL
	icing (confectioner's) sugar	
2 cups	whipping cream	500 mL
1 tbsp.	icing (confectioner's) sugar	15 mL
1 tsp.	vanilla extract	5 mL
2 cups	sliced strawberries	500 mL

- Line a 10 x 15 in. (25 x 38 cm) jelly roll pan with parchment paper.
- In a large bowl, beat egg whites and cream of tartar until frothy. Gradually beat in sugar, beating until stiff peaks form.
- In a medium bowl, beat egg yolks, sugar, water and vanilla until very thick. Sift together flour and salt. Fold dry ingredients into egg yolk mixture until just blended.
- Fold egg yolk mixture into egg white mixture.
- Turn batter into prepared pan, spreading batter evenly to edges.
- Bake at 350°F (180°C) for 15 minutes, or until cake springs back when lightly touched in the center.
- Generously shake icing sugar over cake. Place a clean tea towel on top and turn cake out. Remove parchment paper and sprinkle other side of cake with icing sugar. Cut off any crisp cake edges.
- While still warm, roll cake with towel, beginning at long edge of cake. Set on a cooling rack. When cool, unroll and remove towel.

Jelly Roll with Strawberries and Cream
(Continued)

- In a deep bowl, whip together whipping cream, icing sugar and vanilla extract. Spread about ½ over cake. Top whipped cream with about ½ of strawberries. Re-roll cake; refrigerate.
- To serve, cut into 1" (2.5 cm) slices and garnish with additional whipped cream and strawberries. Sprinkle with additional icing sugar.

VARIATION   ***Chocolate Jelly Roll*** – Substitute ¾ cup (175 mL) cake flour and ¼ cup (60 mL) cocoa for the 1 cup (250 mL) of cake flour.

YIELD   ***8 – 10 SERVINGS***

Apple 'n' Orange Baked Pudding

SERVED WARM WITH ICE CREAM, THIS IS TRULY COMFORT FOOD!

3 tbsp.	brown sugar	45 mL
1 tsp.	ground cinnamon	5 mL
2	oranges, peeled, sliced, quartered	2
3-4	apples, quartered, peeled, cored, sliced	3-4
1 cup	all-purpose flour	250 mL
¾ cup	sugar	175 mL
1 tsp.	baking powder	5 mL
¼ tsp.	salt	1 mL
1 tsp.	freshly grated orange zest	5 mL
1	egg, beaten	1
2 tbsp.	butter, melted	30 mL
½ cup	orange juice	125 mL

- In a small bowl, combine sugar and cinnamon.
- In a lightly buttered, 10-cup (2.5 L) casserole, arrange orange and apple slices. Sprinkle with ½ the brown sugar mixture.
- In a small bowl, combine flour, sugar, baking powder, salt and orange zest. Add egg; mix until crumbly. Spread evenly over fruit. Sprinkle with remaining brown sugar. Drizzle with butter and orange juice.
- Bake at 350°F (180°C) for 50-60 minutes. Serve warm or cold.

YIELD   ***6 – 8 SERVINGS***

CARROT & POTATO STEAMED PUDDING

A MOIST CHRISTMAS PUDDING – LIGHTER THAN THE SUET-BASED PLUM PUDDING

1 cup	EACH raisins & currants	250 mL
½ cup	candied mixed peel	125 mL
1 cup	all-purpose flour	250 mL
½ tsp.	EACH ground cloves, nutmeg, cinnamon	2 mL
½ cup	butter	125 mL
1 cup	brown sugar	250 mL
1	egg	1
1 cup	grated carrot	250 mL
1 cup	grated potato	250 mL
1 tsp.	baking soda	5 mL

- In a medium bowl, combine raisins, currants and peel. Sift together flour, cloves, nutmeg and cinnamon; add to the fruit. Combine well.
- In a large bowl, cream butter and sugar. Blend in egg. Add carrot and half the potato. Add fruit mixture and mix well.
- Add baking soda to remaining half of the potato. Stir well; add to fruit.
- Spoon batter into a well-buttered 6-cup (1.5 L) pudding mold or pudding bowl. Tightly cover the mold with a buttered lid. If using a pudding bowl, cover tightly with a buttered double layer of foil. Tie foil with string.
- To steam pudding, place mold on a rack or trivet in a Dutch oven or a large pot with a close-fitting lid. Add enough water around sides of pudding to come halfway up sides of mold. Cover pot.
- Simmer for 2½ hours, adding additional water if necessary. Remove mold to a cooling rack. Let sit for 10 minutes before unmolding to cool completely. Refrigerate for up to 1 week or freeze.
- To serve, reheat by steaming in mold for 1 hour. Small servings can be heated in a microwave. Serve with warm Orange Sauce, page 163.

YIELD   12 SERVINGS

ORANGE SAUCE

1½ cups	milk	375 mL
1 cup	sugar	250 mL
2 tbsp.	cornstarch	30 mL
¼ cup	butter	60 mL
2 tbsp.	orange liqueur	30 mL
1 tsp.	clear vanilla extract	5 mL
1	egg yolk	1

- In a saucepan, combine milk, sugar, cornstarch and butter. Cook over medium-high heat, stirring until mixture begins to thicken.
- In a small bowl, whisk together liqueur, vanilla and egg yolk. Stir 3 tbsp. (45 mL) of hot milk mixture into egg yolk mixture. Add to hot milk. Cook over medium heat until sauce begins to bubble.

YIELD   *2 CUPS (500 ML) OF SAUCE*

BLUEBERRY PUDDING

SERVE WARM WITH WHIPPED CREAM OR ICE CREAM

3 cups	fresh blueberries	750 mL
2 tbsp.	lemon juice	30 mL
1½ cups	flour	375 mL
2 cups	sugar, divided	500 mL
1½ tsp.	baking powder	7 mL
¾ cup	milk	175 mL
3 tbsp.	butter, melted	45 mL
5 tsp.	cornstarch	25 mL
1½ cups	boiling water	375 mL

- Place blueberries in a greased 10-cup (2.5 L) or larger ovenproof casserole. Sprinkle with lemon juice.
- In a medium bowl, combine flour, 1 cup (250 mL) sugar and baking powder. Add milk and butter; mix well. Spoon batter over berries.
- In a small bowl, combine remaining 1 cup (250 mL) of sugar with cornstarch; sprinkle over batter. Slowly pour boiling water over all.
- Bake at 350°F (180°C) for 50 minutes, or until batter tests done.

YIELD   *6 SERVINGS*

FRESH STRAWBERRY CREAM TART

SO BEAUTIFUL GUESTS WILL THINK YOU'VE BEEN TO THE PÂTISSERIE

CRUMB CRUST:

1 cup	graham or chocolate wafer crumbs	250 mL
1 tbsp.	sugar	15 mL
¼ cup	butter, melted	60 mL

VANILLA CREAM FILLING:

6 oz.	cream cheese	170 g
¼ cup	icing (confectioner's) sugar	60 mL
1 tsp.	vanilla extract	5 mL

FRESH STRAWBERRY TOPPING:

6 cups	strawberries	1.5 L
⅔ cup	sugar	150 mL
1 tbsp.	cornstarch	15 mL
1 tbsp.	lemon juice	15 mL

- **For crust**, combine all crust ingredients. Press crumbs into the bottom and up the sides of a lightly greased 9" (23 cm) tart/flan pan with a removable bottom. Bake at 350°F (180°C) for 8 minutes. Cool.
- Beat together filling ingredients; spread over cooled crust.
- Hull and wash strawberries. Slice off the top ⅓ of each strawberry. Arrange strawberry tips, points up, in a circular pattern over the filling.
- **For glaze**, purée the sliced-off strawberry tops. Place puréed strawberries, sugar, cornstarch and lemon juice in a saucepan over medium heat. Bring to a boil while stirring. Reduce heat to low; cook for 1 minute. Remove from heat; stir until cool. Drizzle glaze over strawberries. Cover and chill before serving.

YIELD   8 SERVINGS

FRESH RASPBERRY PIE

ABSOLUTELY LUSCIOUS – A PERFECT PRESENTATION FOR FRESH SEASONAL FRUIT

1	9" (23 cm) baked graham wafer pie crust, see page 164, chilled	1
3 cups	fresh raspberries	750 mL
1½ cups	water	375 mL
¾ cup	sugar	175 mL
2 tbsp.	golden corn syrup	30 mL
3 oz.	pkg. raspberry gelatin	85 g
2 tbsp.	cornstarch	30 mL
½ tsp.	vanilla extract	2 mL

- Arrange raspberries in pie crust.
- In a small saucepan, combine remaining ingredients. Bring to a boil while stirring. Cool until glaze just begins to set. Pour over raspberries. Cool.
- If you wish, serve with a dollop of whipped cream or a scoop of ice cream.

VARIATION For **Fresh Fruit Pies**, substitute strawberries, blueberries, or peaches for the raspberries and replace raspberry gelatin with the appropriate flavor.

YIELD **6 SERVINGS**

 Sweet and tart, raspberries have an intense flavor. They come in red, yellow and black varieties, but the red are the most popular. Plump, ripe berries should have no hulls attached. Store in a single layer in the refrigerator for 2-3 days. Rinse only if necessary. Fresh is best, but they do freeze well and make excellent jams and jellies. Raspberries contain vitamins A and C, plus iron and potassium.

SOUR CREAM RAISIN MERINGUE PIE

A PRAIRIE TRADITION – FIRST CHOICE AT CHURCH SUPPERS

1½ cups	golden raisins	375 mL
½ cup	sugar	125 mL
¼ cup	cornstarch	60 mL
½ tsp.	cinnamon	2 mL
¼ tsp.	nutmeg	1 mL
¼ tsp.	salt	1 mL
1½ cups	milk	375 mL
3	egg yolks, beaten	3
½ cup	sour cream	125 mL
1 tbsp.	lemon juice	15 mL
1	9" (23 cm) baked pie shell*	1

MERINGUE:

3	egg whites	3
¼ cup	sugar	60 mL
½ tsp.	cream of tartar	2 mL

- **For filling**, in a medium saucepan, combine raisins, sugar, cornstarch, cinnamon, nutmeg and salt; mix well. Stir in milk; blend until smooth. Over medium heat, stir and cook until boiling. Boil 1 minute; remove from heat.
- Stir a small amount of raisin mixture into egg yolks. Return to raisin mixture. Add sour cream; mix well. Cook, stirring constantly, just until filling bubbles. Remove from heat.
- Add lemon juice; mix well. Cool.
- Pour cooled raisin filling into pie shell. Cool.
- **For meringue**, beat egg whites until fluffy. Continue to beat, gradually adding sugar and cream of tartar. Beat until stiff peaks form. Spread meringue over cooled pie filling, sealing edges. Bake pie at 350°F (180°C) for 10 minutes, or until meringue is lightly browned.

NOTE   Seal meringue to all edges of the pie crust to prevent shrinking.

* Use pie pastry on page 133 of *Grandma's Touch* or use your favorite pastry.

YIELD   **6 SERVINGS**

PECAN PRALINE TART

VERY RICH – OUTRAGEOUSLY GOOD

SWEET PIE CRUST (PÂTE SUCRÉE):

½ cup	butter, softened	125 mL
½ cup	sugar	125 mL
1	egg	1
1½ cups	all-purpose flour	375 mL
1 tsp.	vanilla extract	5 mL

PECAN PRALINE FILLING:

2 cups	coarsely chopped pecans	500 mL
1 cup	brown sugar	250 mL
⅓ cup	butter	75 mL
⅓ cup	corn syrup	75 mL
3 tbsp.	whipping cream	45 mL
1 tsp.	vanilla extract	5 mL

- **For crust**, in a medium bowl, cream butter with sugar. Add egg; mix well. Add flour; mix just until blended and crumbly. Press crust crumbs onto the bottom and up the sides of an ungreased 11" (28 cm) tart/flan pan with a removable bottom. Bake at 375°F (190°C) for 12-15 minutes. or until golden. Cool.
- **For filling**, sprinkle chopped nuts over cooled crust. In a small saucepan, combine sugar, butter, corn syrup and whipping cream. Bring to a boil, stirring for 1 minute. Remove from heat; add vanilla. Pour hot syrup over pecans. Bake at 375°F (190°C) for 12-15 minutes, or until filling is bubbly. Cool.
- If you wish, serve with a dollop of whipped cream or a scoop of ice cream.

YIELD   *12 SERVINGS*

MASCARPONE STRAWBERRY CHEESECAKE

MASCARPONE MAKES AN INCREDIBLY CREAMY CHEESECAKE

CRUMB CRUST:

1½ cups	ladyfinger biscuit crumbs	375 mL
2 tbsp.	sugar	30 mL
3 tbsp.	melted butter	45 ml

MASCARPONE FILLING:

1½ cups	mascarpone cheese	375 mL
½ cup	sugar	125 mL
2	eggs	2
1 tbsp.	lemon juice	15 mL
1 tbsp.	grated lemon zest	15 mL
1 tsp.	vanilla extract	5 mL
3 tbsp.	all-purpose flour	45 mL
¼ tsp.	salt	1 mL

STRAWBERRY TOPPING:

1 lb.	strawberries, hulled, sliced	500 g
2 tbsp.	sugar	30 mL
2 tbsp.	strawberry OR orange liqueur	30 mL

- **For crust**, combine all ingredients. Press into bottom and ¾" (2 cm) up sides of a lightly greased 9" (23 cm) springform pan. Bake at 350°F (180°C) for 10-12 minutes, or until crisp and golden. Cool.
- **For filling**, in a medium bowl, beat cheese and sugar until smooth. Add eggs, 1 at a time; beat well after each. Add lemon juice, zest and vanilla; beat well. Combine flour and salt; blend into cheese mixture.
- Pour filling into cooled crust. Bake at 350°F (180°C) for 35-40 minutes, until lightly golden and firm. Cool.
- Remove cheesecake from pan; refrigerate at least 6 hours before serving.
- **For topping**, combine sliced strawberries, sugar and liqueur. Chill.
- To serve, cut cheesecake into wedges; garnish with strawberries.

VARIATION   Substitute ¼ cup (60 mL) balsamic vinegar for the liqueur. Increase sugar to ½ cup (125 mL), or to taste.

YIELD   **8 – 10 SERVINGS**

PUMPKIN CHEESECAKE

START A NEW THANKSGIVING TRADITION

1¼ cups	gingersnap OR graham wafer crumbs	300 mL
⅓ cup	butter, melted	75 mL
2 x 8 oz.	pkgs. cream cheese	2 x 250 g
½ cup	sugar	125 mL
1 tsp.	vanilla extract	5 mL
2	eggs	2
½ cup	canned pure pumpkin	125 mL
½ tsp.	cinnamon	2 mL
¼ tsp.	EACH cloves, nutmeg, ginger & allspice	1 mL

VANILLA CREAM TOPPING:

1 cup	whipping cream	250 mL
1 tbsp.	icing (confectioner's) sugar	15 mL
1 tsp.	vanilla extract	5 mL

- Combine crumbs and melted butter. Press into the bottom and 1" (2.5 cm) up the sides of a 9" (23 cm) springform pan.
- In a large bowl, beat cream cheese, sugar and vanilla until well blended. Add eggs, pumpkin and spices; beat until smooth. Pour into crust.
- Bake at 350°F (180°C) for 40 minutes, or until center is just set. Cool; refrigerate for a few hours.
- Beat topping ingredients together until cream is whipped. Serve cheesecake topped with a dollop of whipped cream

YIELD   8 – 10 SERVINGS

 For moist cheesecakes that don't crack or sag when cooled, wrap outside of springform pan in heavy-duty foil before adding crust and filling. To bake, place filled pan in a larger pan and add hot water to come halfway up the sides of the springform pan.

DAFFODIL CAKE

A GREAT CAKE FOR EASTER, MOTHER'S DAY OR ANY SPECIAL OCCASION!

WHITE BATTER:

6	egg whites, room temperature	6
½ tsp.	cream of tartar	2 mL
½ tsp.	clear vanilla extract	2 mL
¼ tsp.	salt	1 mL
½ cup	sugar	125 mL
½ cup	cake flour	125 mL
½ cup	icing (confectioner's) sugar	125 mL

YELLOW BATTER:

6	egg yolks	6
2 tbsp.	lemon juice	30 mL
1 tbsp.	cold water	15 mL
½ tsp.	lemon extract	2 mL
½ cup	sugar	125 mL
¾ cup	cake flour	175 mL
1 tsp.	baking powder	5 mL
¼ tsp.	salt	1 mL

- **For white batter**, in a large bowl, beat egg whites until frothy. Add cream of tartar, vanilla and salt; continue to beat until soft peaks form. While beating, gradually add sugar; beat until stiff peaks form.
- Sift flour and icing sugar; fold into egg whites ¼ at a time.
- **For yellow batter**, in a large bowl, beat egg yolks, lemon juice, water and lemon extract until mixture is thick, about 5 minutes. While beating, gradually add sugar.
- Sift flour, baking powder and salt; fold into yolk mixture ¼ at a time.
- Alternately spoon white and yellow batters into an ungreased 10" (25 cm) tube pan. Bake at 350°F (180°C) for 1 hour.
- Invert on a funnel until cool; remove from pan. Dust cake with icing sugar or frost with Cream Cheese Frosting, see page 174.

YIELD   **12 SERVINGS**

HONEY CAKE (MEDIVNYK)

A TREASURED RECIPE IN UKRAINIAN AND JEWISH HOMES

4	eggs, separated	4
1 cup	sugar	250 mL
¼ cup	vegetable oil	60 mL
1 cup	liquid honey	250 mL
1 cup	strong coffee	250 mL
1 tsp.	baking soda	5 mL
3 cups	all-purpose flour	750 mL
1 tsp.	baking powder	5 mL
½ tsp.	salt	2 mL
1 tsp.	EACH cinnamon & allspice	5 mL
½ cup	chopped nuts (walnuts, pecans, almonds)	125 mL

- Beat egg whites until stiff; set aside.
- In a large bowl, beat egg yolks until light. Add sugar, oil and honey; beat well.
- In a small bowl, combine coffee and baking soda.
- Sift dry ingredients together, except for nuts. Add to honey mixture alternately with coffee. Stir in nuts.
- Fold egg whites into batter.
- Pour batter into a greased and floured 12-cup (3 L) bundt pan.
- Bake at 325°F (160°C) for an hour, or until cake tester comes out clean.
- Cool for 7 minutes on a rack; turn out of pan; cool.
- Let cake age for 2-3 days before serving.

VARIATION	Add grated rind and juice of 1 orange to honey mixture – reduce coffee to ½ cup (125 mL). Add 1 tsp. (5 mL) ground ginger OR ½ cup (125 mL) finely chopped crystallized ginger. Dust cake with icing sugar before serving.
NOTE	To measure honey, first coat measuring cup or spoon with vegetable oil – the honey will pour easily.
YIELD	*16 – 20 SERVINGS*

APPLE CAKE WITH VANILLA SAUCE

APPLE PIE FLAVORS WITH A BUTTERY VANILLA SAUCE

¾ cup	applesauce	175 mL
¾ cup	vegetable oil	175 mL
2	eggs	2
1 tbsp.	cinnamon	15 mL
1 tsp.	nutmeg	5 mL
1½ cups	sugar	375 mL
2 tsp.	vanilla extract	10 mL
3 cups	all-purpose flour	750 mL
½ tsp.	salt	2 mL
1½ tsp.	baking soda	7 mL
4	medium-sized apples, grated	4

VANILLA SAUCE:

1 cup	sugar	250 mL
2 tbsp.	cornstarch	30 mL
2 cups	water	500 mL
¼ cup	butter	60 mL
2 tsp.	vanilla extract	10 mL

- In a large bowl, combine applesauce, oil, eggs, cinnamon, nutmeg, sugar and vanilla. Mix well.
- In a medium bowl, sift flour, salt and baking soda together. Add to the applesauce mixture. Add grated apples.
- Pour batter into a greased and floured 10" (25 cm) bundt pan. Bake at 350°F (180°C) for 50 minutes, or until a cake tester comes out clean.
- Cool on a rack for 10 minutes. Turn out; cool.
- **For sauce**, in a small saucepan, whisk together sugar and cornstarch. Whisk in water gradually. Bring to a boil over medium-high heat. Boil for 1 minute, stirring constantly. Remove from heat. Whisk in butter and vanilla. Serve warm over cooled cake.

YIELD   *12 – 16 SERVINGS*

CARROT PECAN CAKE

THE BLENDER METHOD MAKES THIS A SNAP

1 cup	pecan halves	250 mL
¾ cup	unsweetened applesauce	175 mL
½ cup	vegetable oil	125 mL
4	eggs	4
1 cup	brown sugar	250 mL
2 tsp.	ground cinnamon	10 mL
1 tsp.	salt	5 mL
3 cups	sliced raw carrots	750 mL
2 cups	all-purpose flour	500 mL
1 tsp.	baking soda	5 mL
2 tsp.	baking powder	10 mL
1 cup	raisins	250 mL

- Finely chop pecans in blender and set aside.
- Place applesauce, oil, eggs, sugar, cinnamon and salt in blender. Blend for 5 seconds. Gradually add carrots; blend until grated.
- In a large bowl, sift flour, baking soda and baking powder. Pour the liquid ingredients over the dry ingredients; mix well. Mix in pecans and raisins.
- Pour batter into a greased and floured 10-cup bundt pan or 10" (25 cm) tube pan.
- Bake at 350°F (180°C) for 1 hour, or until a cake tester comes out clean.
- Frost with an Orange Cream Cheese Frosting (add 1-2 tsp. [5-10 mL] orange juice concentrate to Cream Cheese Frosting, page 174), or with a Butter-Pecan Cream Cheese Frosting (add butter-pecan flavoring to Cream Cheese Frosting), garnished with pecan halves.

YIELD   *16 – 20 PIECES*

PUMPKIN SPICE CAKE

MOIST, DENSE AND DELICIOUS

½ cup	butter, softened	125 mL
½ cup	EACH brown & white sugar	125 mL
3	eggs	3
2 tsp.	vanilla extract	10 mL
2½ cups	all-purpose flour	625 mL
2 tsp.	baking powder	10 mL
1 tsp.	baking soda	5 mL
1½ tsp.	ground cinnamon	7 mL
1 tsp.	nutmeg	5 mL
¼ tsp.	salt	1 mL
2 cups	puréed cooked pumpkin OR 14 oz. (398 mL) canned	500 mL
½ cup	orange marmalade OR apricot jam	125 mL

CREAM CHEESE FROSTING:

4 oz.	cream cheese, softened	115 g
¼ cup	butter, softened	60 mL
1 tsp.	vanilla extract	5 mL
1½ cups	icing (confectioner's) sugar	375 mL

- In a large bowl, cream butter, sugars, eggs and vanilla until fluffy.
- In a small bowl, sift together dry ingredients. Beat dry ingredients alternately with pumpkin into creamed mixture. Blend well.
- Spoon batter into 2 greased, floured 8 or 9" (20 or 23 cm) round cake pans. Bake at 350°F (180°C) for 20-25 minutes 9" (23 cm) pan, 25-30 minutes 8" (20 cm) pan, or until a cake tester comes out clean. Cool on cooling racks for 10 minutes. Remove cake from pans; cool completely.
- **For icing**, beat all ingredients together until creamy.
- To assemble cake, spread marmalade on bottom layer; place second layer on top. Spread icing over sides and top of cake.

YIELD   12 SERVINGS

See photograph opposite.

DESSERTS

Pumpkin Spice Cake, page 174,
    decorated with sliced crystallized ginger
Crackle Ginger Sparklers, page 187

MOCHA CAKE

A "MELT-IN-YOUR-MOUTH" COFFEE AND CHOCOLATE COMBINATION

1½ cups	hot strong coffee	375 mL
½ cup	butter, cubed	125 mL
2 cups	semi-sweet chocolate chips	500 mL
¾ cup	sugar	175 mL
2 cups	all-purpose flour	500 mL
1 tsp.	baking soda	5 mL
2	eggs	2
1 tsp.	vanilla extract	5 mL
	icing (confectioner's) sugar	

- Pour coffee into a medium bowl. Stir in butter and chocolate chips until smooth. Stir in sugar; let cool for 5 minutes.
- Blend flour and baking soda into chocolate mixture. Add eggs and vanilla; beat until well blended.
- Pour batter into a well-greased 10-cup (2.5 L) bundt pan.
- Bake at 325°F (180°C) for 45 minutes, or until a cake tester comes out clean.
- Cool, upright, for 20 minutes. Unmold onto a cooling rack. Cool completely.
- To serve, sprinkle with icing sugar.

YIELD   12 – 16 SERVINGS

IRISH POTATO FUDGE CAKE

AN IRISHMAN'S DREAM – POTATOES MAKE THIS CAKE VERY MOIST

1 cup	butter, softened	250 mL
2 cups	sugar	500 mL
2 oz.	unsweetened chocolate, melted	55 g
1 cup	grated raw potato	250 mL
2 tsp.	vanilla extract	10 mL
½ cup	chopped almonds	125 mL
4	eggs	4
2¼ cups	cake and pastry flour	550 mL
1 tsp.	EACH baking soda & cream of tartar	5 mL
½ tsp.	salt	2 mL
½ tsp.	EACH allspice, cloves & cinnamon	2 mL
½ cup	milk	125 mL

CHOCOLATE FROSTING:

¼ cup	butter	60 mL
2 oz.	unsweetened chocolate	55 g
⅓ cup	cooked mashed potatoes	75 mL
⅛ tsp.	salt	0.5 mL
2 tsp.	vanilla extract	10 mL
2-2½ cups	icing (confectioner's) sugar	500-625 mL

- In a large bowl, cream butter with sugar. Add chocolate, potato, vanilla and almonds. Beat in eggs, 1 at a time.
- Sift dry ingredients together. Add to creamed mixture alternately with the milk.
- Pour batter into a greased 9 x 13" (23 x 33 cm) cake pan.
- Bake at 350°F (180°C) for 50 minutes, or until cake tester comes out clean. Cool.
- **For frosting**, in a small saucepan, over low heat, melt butter. Cook until lightly browned. Stir in chocolate until melted. Remove from heat.
- Stir in potatoes, salt and vanilla. Mix well. Cool to room temperature.
- Stir in sugar to desired consistency. Frost cooled cake.

YIELD   12 SERVINGS

LUMBERJACK CAKE

NUTRITIOUS, SUBSTANTIAL AND SATISFYING.

1 cup	water	250 mL
1 cup	chopped pitted dates	250 mL
1	cooking apple, cored, peeled, chopped	1
1 tsp.	baking soda	5 mL
½ cup	butter, softened	125 mL
1 cup	sugar	250 mL
1	egg	1
1 tsp.	vanilla extract	5 mL
1½ cups	all-purpose flour	375 mL
½ tsp.	salt	2 mL

COCONUT CARAMEL TOPPING:

¼ cup	milk	60 mL
¼ cup	butter	60 mL
½ cup	brown sugar	125 mL
1 cup	medium unsweetened shredded coconut	250 mL
⅓ cup	chopped pecans (optional)	75 mL

- In a small saucepan, over medium heat, bring water to a boil. Add dates and apples; cook for 1 minute. Remove from heat. Add baking soda; mix well. Cool.
- In a large bowl, combine butter and sugar. Stir in egg and vanilla.
- Sift flour and salt. Add to creamed mixture alternately with fruit mixture. Pour batter into a lightly greased 9" (23 cm) square baking pan.
- Bake at 350°F (180°C) for 40 minutes, or until cake springs back when lightly touched.
- While cake is baking, in a small saucepan over low heat, combine topping ingredients. Stir until butter and sugar are melted. Spread topping over baked cake. Broil until topping is golden brown.

YIELD   *12 SERVINGS*

OATMEAL RAISIN SPICE CAKE

CARAMEL FROSTING ADDS THE FINISHING TOUCH

½ cup	quick oat flakes	125 mL
1 cup	boiling water	250 mL
2	eggs	2
1 cup	sugar	250 mL
½ cup	butter OR margarine, softened	125 mL
1 cup	all-purpose flour	250 mL
1 tsp.	ground cinnamon	5 mL
½ tsp.	ground cloves	2 mL
1 tsp.	baking soda	5 mL
½ tsp.	baking powder	2 mL
1 cup	raisins	250 mL
½ cup	unsweetened shredded coconut	125 mL
1 cup	chopped pecans (optional)	250 mL

CARAMEL FROSTING:

¼ cup	butter	60 mL
½ cup	brown sugar	125 mL
2 tbsp.	milk	30 mL
¾ cup	icing (confectioner's) sugar	175 mL

- Place oat flakes in a small bowl. Stir in water; let cool.
- In a large bowl, beat eggs, sugar and butter. Add oats; mix well.
- Sift together flour, cinnamon, cloves, baking soda and baking powder. Add to oat mixture. Beat well.
- Stir in raisins, coconut and pecans.
- Pour batter into a greased 9" (22 cm) square cake pan. Bake at 350°F (180°C) for 30 minutes. Cool.
- **For frosting**, in a small saucepan, combine butter and sugar. Cook over medium heat until bubbles appear. Add milk. Cook for 2 minutes. Remove from heat; stir to cool slightly.
- Add icing sugar until of spreading consistency. Spread on cooled cake.

YIELD   *12 SERVINGS*

"SURFACE OF THE MOON" CAKE

VISUALLY FASCINATING WITH ITS CRATERS AND MOUNTAINS

1 cup	butter OR margarine	250 mL
1 cup	sugar	250 mL
2	eggs, beaten	2
1 tsp.	vanilla extract	5 mL
3	ripe bananas, mashed	3
3 cups	all-purpose flour	750 mL
2 tsp.	baking soda	10 mL
2 tsp.	baking powder	10 mL
1 cup	sour cream (regular or fat-free)	250 mL
½ cup	brown sugar	125 mL
2 tsp.	cinnamon	10 mL
1 cup	chocolate chips	250 mL

- In a large bowl, cream butter, sugar and eggs. Beat until smooth.
- Add vanilla and bananas. Mix until well blended.
- In a small bowl, combine flour, baking soda and baking powder. Add dry ingredients to banana mixture alternately with sour cream, beginning and ending with dry ingredients.
- Grease a 9 x 13" (23 x 33 cm) cake pan. Pour ½ of batter into pan. Combine brown sugar and cinnamon. Sprinkle ½ of brown sugar mixture over batter. Sprinkle with ½ of the chocolate chips. Repeat layers with remaining batter, sugar mixture and chocolate chips.
- Bake at 350°F (180°C) for 40 to 50 minutes.
- Serve warm with a dollop of whipped cream or cold with fresh fruit in season.

YIELD   *12 SERVINGS*

POUND CAKE

BUTTERY FINE-TEXTURED POUND CAKE IS THE BASIS FOR TRIFLES, MANY FRUIT DESSERTS AND IS IDEAL FOR CHOCOLATE FONDUE DIPPING

1 cup	butter, softened	250 mL
2 cups	sugar	500 mL
3½ cups	cake flour	875 mL
1¼ cups	milk	300 mL
1½ tsp.	baking powder	7 mL
2 tsp.	lemon OR vanilla extract	10 mL
⅛ tsp.	salt	0.5 mL
6	egg yolks	6

- In a large bowl, beat butter and sugar until light and fluffy. Add remaining ingredients. Beat for 2-3 minutes, until well mixed, stopping occasionally to scrape bowl with a rubber spatula.
- Spoon batter into a well-greased and floured 10" (25 cm) Bundt pan or 2, 9 x 5" (2 L) loaf pans. Bake at 350°F (180°C) for 1 hour, if using the Bundt pan, or 45 minutes, if using loaf pans. Remove from the oven when a cake tester comes out clean.
- Cool on a wire rack for 10 minutes; turn out to cool completely.

VARIATIONS For **Lemon Poppy Seed Pound Cake**, add 3 tbsp. (45 mL) of poppy seeds and 1 tbsp. (15 mL) grated lemon zest to the batter.

For **Citrus Pound Cake**, use lemon extract and add 1½ tsp. (7 mL) EACH grated orange and lemon zest.

For a **Liqueur Glaze**, combine 1 cup (250 mL) sugar, ½ cup (125 mL) water and ¼ cup (60 mL) corn syrup. Bring to a boil, stirring constantly. Cover and boil for 1-2 minutes. Set aside, uncover and do NOT stir. Let cool for 5 minutes. Stir in ½ cup (125 mL) of Grand Marnier, Cointreau OR Brandy (or rum). With a skewer, poke holes in warm cake while still in pan. Pour liqueur syrup evenly over cake. Let cool in pan for 20-30 minutes, then turn out.

NOTE Tightly wrapped, this cake will retain its freshness for 3 days at room temperature, 1 week in the refrigerator, or 2 months in the freezer.

YIELD **1 BUNDT CAKE OR 2 LOAVES**

CORNMEAL FRUIT CAKE

CORNMEAL ADDS GOLDEN COLOR AND A SLIGHTLY CRUNCHY TEXTURE

1¾ cups	milk	425 mL
1 cup	cornmeal	250 mL
1 tsp.	grated orange rind	5 mL
1 cup	sugar	250 mL
½ cup	currants	125 mL
½ cup	chopped dried apricots	125 mL
2 tbsp.	orange liqueur OR orange juice	30 mL
½ cup	butter	125 mL
½ cup	sugar	125 mL
2	eggs	2
1½ cups	all-purpose flour	375 mL
2½ tsp.	baking powder	12 mL
¼ tsp.	salt	1 mL
	icing (confectioner's) sugar (optional)	

- In a small saucepan, combine milk, cornmeal, orange rind and 1 cup (250 mL) of sugar. Bring to a boil; simmer and stir for 4 minutes, or until mixture is soft and thick. Cool.
- In a medium bowl, combine currants and apricots. Sprinkle with orange liqueur.
- In a large bowl, beat butter with ½ cup (125 mL) sugar until light and fluffy. Beat in eggs, 1 at a time.
- Sift together flour, baking powder and salt. Add to fruit mixture.
- Add cornmeal mixture and flour mixture to creamed butter; mix well.
- Spoon batter into a lightly greased parchment-lined 9" (23 cm) spring-form pan.
- Bake at 350°F (180°C) for 1 hour.
- Let stand for 5 minutes before removing from pan to a wire rack to cool.
- If desired, dust lightly with icing sugar.

YIELD   **12 – 16 SERVINGS**

HUNGARIAN WALNUT COOKIES

THESE SHORTBREAD-LIKE MOLDED COOKIES ARE SPECTACULAR ON ANY PASTRY TRAY. IF YOU CAN'T FIND THE WALNUT-SHAPED COOKIE MOLDS, SHAPE DOUGH INTO SMALL BALLS AND PRESS ONTO COOKIE SHEET TO FLATTEN ONE SIDE.

1 cup	butter, softened	250 mL
½ cup	icing (confectioner's) sugar	125 mL
2 cups	all-purpose flour	500 mL
⅛ tsp.	baking powder	0.5 mL
3½ oz.	walnuts, ground	100 g

COCOA BUTTER FILLING:

1 tbsp.	butter, softened	15 mL
2 tbsp.	cocoa	30 mL
½ cup	icing (confectioner's) sugar	125 mL
2 tsp.	milk	10 mL

- Combine butter and sugar until smooth and creamy.
- Sift together flour and baking powder; add ground walnuts. Stir into creamed mixture.
- Press dough into greased half-walnut-shaped depressions in cookie pan. Bake at 350°F (180°C) for 10 minutes, or until lightly browned around the edges. Cool for 5 minutes. Remove from pan; cool completely.
- **For filling**, combine all filling ingredients until of a thick, spreading consistency.
- Spread filling on flat side of walnut-half-shaped cookie. Press the flat side of another cookie against filling.

YIELD   *3 DOZEN COOKIES*

PRIZE SHORTBREAD

YOU MAY ALSO ADD ALMONDS OR COOKIE DECORATIONS BEFORE BAKING

1 cup	unsalted butter, softened	250 mL
½ cup	icing (confectioner's) sugar	125 mL
¼ tsp.	salt	1 mL
1	egg yolk	1
2 cups	all-purpose flour	500 mL

- In a medium bowl, cream butter. Add sugar and combine thoroughly. Add salt and egg yolk; mix well.
- Add flour in 4 portions, mixing well after each addition.
- Turn dough, in small portions, onto a lightly floured surface. Roll to ⅛" (3 mm) thickness. Cut out cookies with lightly floured cookie cutters. Transfer cookies to ungreased cookie sheets.
- Bake at 300°F (150°C) for 10 minutes, or until cookies just begin to brown. Remove cookies to cooling racks.

YIELD   *4 DOZEN COOKIES*

BROWN SUGAR SHORTBREAD

RICH FLAVOR – BUTTERY TEXTURE

1 lb.	unsalted butter, softened	454 g
1 cup	golden sugar	250 mL
½ tsp.	vanilla extract	2 mL
4 cups	all-purpose flour	1 L

- In a large bowl, cream butter with sugar. Add vanilla and mix well.
- Add flour in 4 portions, mixing well after each addition.
- Turn dough onto a lightly floured surface and knead until all cracks in dough disappear.
- Press dough into an ungreased 9 x 13" (23 x 33 cm) baking pan. Prick dough deeply with a fork.
- Bake at 350°F (180°C) for 20-25 minutes. Cut into squares. Cool.

YIELD   *48 SQUARES*

YOGURT PECAN DROP COOKIES

A GREAT BASIC COOKIE WITH DELICIOUS VARIATIONS

¾ cup	packed brown sugar	175 mL
½ cup	sugar	125 mL
½ cup	butter OR margarine, softened	125 mL
½ cup	vegetable shortening OR vegetable oil	125 mL
2 tsp.	vanilla	10 mL
1	egg	1
1¾ cups	all-purpose flour	425 mL
1 tsp.	baking soda	5 mL
½ tsp.	salt	2 mL
1 cup	yogurt chips	250 mL
½ cup	chopped pecans	125 mL

- In a large bowl, combine sugars, butter and shortening. Beat until light and fluffy. Add vanilla and egg. Blend well.
- In a small bowl, sift together flour, baking soda and salt. Add dry ingredients to creamed mixture; mix well. Stir in yogurt chips and nuts.
- Using a tablespoon-sized (15 mL) scoop, drop dough onto parchment-lined cookie sheets, leaving room for spreading.
- Bake at 350°F (180°C) for 10 minutes, or until cookies are just lightly golden brown.
- Remove cookie sheet from oven and place on a cooking rack for 1-2 minutes before removing cookies to cooling rack.

VARIATION   Substitute chocolate, butterscotch, or peanut butter chips, caramel bits, mini Smarties and chopped walnuts or almonds for the yogurt chips and pecans. Substitute vanilla with other extracts which complement the selected ingredients.

NOTE   These cookies freeze well and only require a few minutes to defrost.

YIELD   *4 DOZEN 2" (5 CM) COOKIES*

CRACKLE GINGER SPARKLERS

SUGAR LIGHTS UP THE TOPS OF THESE ZESTY GINGER COOKIES

¾ cup	butter OR margarine	175 mL
1 cup	brown sugar	250 mL
¼ cup	molasses	60 mL
1	egg	1
2 cups	all-purpose flour	500 mL
2 tsp.	baking soda	10 mL
½ tsp.	salt	2 mL
1 tsp.	ginger	5 mL
1 tsp.	cinnamon	5 mL
½ tsp.	cloves	2 mL
	granulated sugar	

- In a large bowl, cream together butter, brown sugar, molasses and egg until light and fluffy.
- In a medium bowl, combine flour, baking soda, salt and spices; stir thoroughly. Add to creamed mixture until well blended.
- Shape into 1" (2.5 cm) balls. Roll in granulated sugar; place 2" (5 cm) apart on greased cookie sheets.
- Bake at 375°F (190°C) for 8-10 minutes. Cool slightly; remove from pan.

VARIATION   For ***Double Ginger Sparklers***, stir ¼-½ cup (60-125 mL) coarsely chopped crystallized ginger into dough just before shaping into balls.

YIELD   ***5 DOZEN COOKIES***

See photograph on page 175.

CHOCOLATE CHOCOLATE CHIP COOKIES

CHOCOLATE LOVERS BEWARE – THESE ARE ADDICTIVE

1 cup	butter OR margarine, softened	250 mL
1½ cups	sugar	375 mL
2	eggs	2
2 tsp.	vanilla extract	10 mL
2 cups	all-purpose flour	500 mL
⅔ cup	cocoa	150 mL
1 tsp.	baking soda	5 mL
¼ tsp.	salt	1 mL
1½ cups	chocolate chips	375 mL

- In a large bowl, beat butter, sugar, eggs and vanilla until light and fluffy.
- Sift together flour, cocoa, baking soda and salt. Add to creamed mixture; blend well. Stir in chocolate chips.
- Drop by tablespoonfuls (15 mL) onto ungreased cookie sheets.
- Bake at 350°F (180°C) for 10 minutes. Cool slightly; remove from cookie sheets to cooling racks. Cool.

YIELD   *5 DOZEN 2" (5 CM) COOKIES*

CHOCO-OAT RAISIN COOKIES

A GREAT AFTER-SCHOOL SNACK WITH A GLASS OF MILK

1 cup	butter OR margarine, softened	250 mL
¾ cup	brown sugar	175 mL
¼ cup	sugar	60 mL
2	eggs	2
1 tsp.	vanilla	5 mL
2 cups	all-purpose flour	500 mL
½ tsp.	salt	2 mL
1 tsp.	baking soda	5 mL
⅓ cup	boiling water	75 mL
2 cups	quick-cooking oat flakes	500 mL
1 cup	EACH raisins & chocolate chips	250 mL

Choco-Oat Raisin Cookies

(Continued)

- In a large bowl, beat butter, sugars, eggs and vanilla. Beat in flour and salt.
- Dissolve baking soda in boiling water; blend into flour mixture.
- Stir in oat flakes, raisins and chocolate chips.
- Drop by tablespoonfuls (15 mL) onto ungreased cookie sheet. Flatten slightly.
- Bake at 350°F (180°C) for 12-15 minutes.

YIELD　　**6 DOZEN 2" (5 CM) COOKIES**

Dad's Cookies

Tried and True – these are hard to beat

1 cup	butter, softened	250 mL
2 cups	brown sugar	500 mL
1 cup	golden corn syrup	250 mL
2	eggs	2
3 cups	all-purpose flour	750 mL
3 cups	rolled oats or quick oats	750 mL
1 tbsp.	baking soda	15 mL
1 tsp.	ground ginger	5 mL
2 tsp.	ground cinnamon	10 mL
pinch	salt	pinch
1 cup	unsweetened flaked coconut	250 mL

- In a large bowl, cream butter, sugar and corn syrup. Beat in eggs.
- In a medium bowl, combine remaining ingredients. Add dry ingredients to creamed mixture. Mix well.
- Drop by tablespoonfuls (15 mL) onto cookie sheets lined with parchment paper.
- Bake at 350°F (180°C) for 10-12 minutes, or until golden.

NOTE　　For uniform cookies, use a tablespoon-size (15 mL) spring-operated scoop.

YIELD　　**8 DOZEN 2½" (6 CM) COOKIES**

CHOCOLATE BUTTERSCOTCH RIPPLE SQUARES

CHEWY AND DELICIOUS – SATISFIES ANY SWEET TOOTH

1½ cups	butterscotch chips	375 mL
10 oz.	can sweetened condensed milk	300 mL
2 tbsp.	butter	30 mL
2 cups	packed brown sugar	500 mL
2	eggs	2
1 cup	butter, melted	250 mL
2 tsp.	vanilla extract	10 mL
1½ cups	all-purpose flour	375 mL
⅔ cup	quick-cooking oat flakes	150 mL
⅓ cup	cocoa	75 mL
1 cup	chopped walnuts OR pecans	250 mL

- In a small saucepan, over low heat, combine chips, milk and 2 tbsp. (30 mL) butter until melted. Set aside.
- In a large bowl, mix brown sugar, eggs, melted butter and vanilla until smooth. Stir in flour, oat flakes, cocoa and nuts. Mix well.
- Pat half of oat mixture into a greased 9 x 13" (23 x 33 cm) baking pan. Spread butterscotch mixture over base. Drop remaining oat mixture by spoonfuls on top of butterscotch layer; spread lightly with a knife to cover filling.
- Bake at 350°F (180°C) for 40 minutes. Cool; cut into squares.

YIELD   24 SQUARES

To make your own **Sweetened Condensed Milk**, place ¼ cup (60 mL) butter or margarine, ⅔ cup (150 mL) sugar, 1 cup (250 mL) instant skim milk powder and ⅓ cup (75 mL) hot water in a blender container. Blend until smooth. Cover and refrigerate overnight before using. Yield is 1⅓ cups (325 mL).

CHOCO-PECAN SQUARES

CARAMELIZED PECANS WITH CHOCOLATE – DECADENT

½ cup	butter OR margarine	125 mL
1 cup	brown sugar	250 mL
2 cups	all-purpose flour	500 mL
1½ cups	pecan halves	375 mL
1 cup	butter	250 mL
¾ cup	brown sugar	175 mL
1 cup	mini chocolate chips	250 mL

- In a medium bowl, combine butter, 1 cup (250 mL) brown sugar and flour until crumbly. Press into an ungreased 9 x 13" (23 x 33 cm) pan.
- Sprinkle pecans over in a single layer.
- In a small saucepan, melt butter and ¾ cup (175 mL) brown sugar. Bring to a boil; cook for 1 minute. Pour over pecan layer.
- Bake at 350°F (180°C) for 25 minutes, or until caramel bubbles in the middle. Remove from oven.
- Sprinkle chocolate chips over caramel layer. Return to oven and bake for 2 minutes. Cool.

VARIATIONS   Substitute butterscotch or peanut butter chips and chopped walnuts or almonds for the chocolate chips and pecans.

YIELD   **30 SQUARES**

 Store shelled pecans for up to 3 months in an airtight container in the refrigerator or freeze for up to 6 months. Because of their high fat content, over 70%, pecans can become rancid quickly. Pecans are among the nuts rich in monounsaturated fat, which helps reduce the level of LDL cholesterol. Pecans are also rich in vitamin E, fiber, calcium, folic acid, potassium and magnesium.

CHEWY GRANOLA BARS

DON'T BE CAUGHT WITHOUT ONE OF THESE BARS IN YOUR BACKPACK,
GLOVE COMPARTMENT, DESK DRAWER, ETC.

1 cup	brown sugar	250 mL
¼ cup	sugar	60 mL
½ cup	butter OR margarine, softened	125 mL
2 tbsp.	light corn syrup OR liquid honey	30 mL
1 tsp.	vanilla extract	5 mL
1	egg	1
1 cup	all-purpose flour	250 mL
½ cup	wheat germ	125 mL
1 tsp.	ground cinnamon	5 mL
½ tsp.	baking powder	2 mL
¼ tsp.	salt	1 mL
1½ cups	quick-cooking oats	375 mL
1¼ cups	crisp rice cereal	300 mL
1 cup	raw sunflower seeds OR chopped nuts	250 mL
1 cup	chocolate, butterscotch, yogurt, OR peanut butter chips	250 mL

- In a large bowl, combine sugars and butter. Beat well.
- Add corn syrup, vanilla and egg; mix well. Blend in flour, wheat germ, cinnamon, baking powder and salt.
- Add remaining ingredients and mix well.
- Press mixture into a 9 x 13" (23 x 33 cm) greased or parchment-lined baking pan. Bake at 350°F (180°C) for 20 minutes, or until edges begin to brown lightly. Remove to a cooling rack.
- When cool, cut into bars.

VARIATIONS   An equal amount of raisins, currants, coconut, etc., may be substituted for the sunflower seeds and chocolate or other chips.

YIELD   *20 BARS*

YUMMY YAM SQUARES

ALSO DELICIOUS USING COOKED MASHED CARROTS OR PUMPKIN

1 cup	all-purpose flour	250 mL
½ cup	quick-cooking rolled oats	125 mL
½ cup	packed brown sugar	125 mL
½ cup	butter, softened	125 mL
2 cups	cooked, mashed yams	500 mL
10 oz.	can sweetened condensed milk, amaretto-flavored	300 mL
2	eggs	2
½ tsp.	salt	2 mL
2 tsp.	pumpkin pie spice*	10 mL
1 cup	sliced almonds	250 mL
½ cup	packed brown sugar	125 mL
2 tbsp.	butter, softened	30 mL
	whipped cream, ice cream	

- In a small bowl, combine flour, oats, brown sugar and butter. Mix until crumbly. Press into an ungreased 9 x 13" (23 x 33 cm) baking pan. Bake at 350°F (180°C) for 15 minutes.
- In a medium bowl, combine yams, milk, eggs, salt and spice. Pour over baked crust. Bake for an additional 20 minutes.
- Combine almonds, brown sugar and butter. Sprinkle over yam mixture. Bake for an additional 20 minutes, or until filling is set.
- Cool on a rack before cutting into squares.

VARIATIONS   1. Use regular sweetened condensed milk; add 1 tsp. (5 mL) butter-pecan extract to filling; substitute chopped pecans for almonds. Also see Sweetened Condensed Milk note on page 190.

                       2. Use regular sweetened condensed milk; add 1 tbsp. (15 mL) Frangelico liqueur; substitute chopped hazelnuts (filberts) for almonds.

NOTE   Make **Pumpkin Pie Spice** by combining 1 tsp. (5 mL) cinnamon, ½ tsp. (2 mL) ginger, ¼ tsp. (1 mL) nutmeg and ¼ tsp. (1 mL) allspice.

YIELD   *24 SQUARES*

RASPBERRY ALMOND SQUARES

BEST-SELLERS AT BAKE SALES – COLORFUL, CRUNCHY AND FLAVORFUL

1¾ cups	all-purpose flour	425 mL
1 cup	sugar	250 mL
1 cup	butter, softened	250 mL
1	egg, lightly beaten	1
1 tsp.	almond extract	5 mL
1 cup	"no-sugar-added" raspberry spread	250 mL
1 cup	white chocolate chips	250 mL
1 cup	sliced almonds	250 mL

- In a large bowl, combine flour and sugar. Cut in butter with a pastry blender until mixture is crumbly. Add egg and almond extract; mix well.
- Set aside 1 cup (250 mL) of crumb mixture. Press remaining crumbs into a lightly greased 9 x 13" (23 x 33 cm) baking pan.
- Spread raspberry spread over base.
- Combine reserved crumbs with chocolate chips and almonds. Spoon over raspberry layer; press down lightly.
- Bake at 350°F (180°C) for 45 minutes, or until top layer is lightly browned.

YIELD   32 SQUARES

 White chocolate contains cocoa butter which gives it a creamy, delicate milk-chocolate flavor. However, it contains no chocolate liquor (cocoa solids), which means that it can not be officially classified as chocolate. Melt white chocolate over very low heat to prevent scorching. It is available in blocks, squares, chunks and chips.

WALNUT SLICE

A HOUSEHOLD FAVORITE FOR OVER THREE GENERATIONS!

½ cup	sugar	125 mL
½ cup	butter, softened	125 mL
2	egg yolks	2
1 tsp.	vanilla extract	5 mL
1½ cups	all-purpose flour	375 mL
1 tsp.	baking powder	5 mL
½ tsp.	salt	2 mL
2	egg whites	2
1 cup	brown sugar	250 mL
1 cup	chopped walnuts	250 mL

- In a large bowl, cream sugar and butter. Add egg yolks and vanilla; mix well.
- Sift flour, baking powder and salt. Add to creamed mixture.
- Spread dough in a lightly greased 9 x 13" (23 x 33 cm) baking pan.
- Beat egg whites until frothy. Add brown sugar; continue to beat until stiff peaks form. Fold in walnuts. Spread over base.
- Bake at 350°F (180°C) for 25 minutes. Cool. Cut into squares.

YIELD   *30 SQUARES*

RICE KRISPIE CHOCOLATE SQUARES

MILLIONAIRES' RICE KRISPIE SQUARES – MAKE THAT A BILLION!

3 x 2 oz.	Mars chocolate bars, chopped	3 x 58 g
¼ cup	butter	60 mL
3 cups	Rice Krispie cereal	750 mL
1 cup	chocolate chips	250 mL
2 tbsp.	peanut butter	30 mL

- In a large saucepan, over low heat, melt chocolate bars and butter. Stir in cereal. Spread into a lightly greased 9" (23 cm) square baking pan.
- In a small saucepan, over low heat, melt chocolate chips and peanut butter. Spread over cereal layer. Cool. Cut into squares.

VARIATION   For **Old-Fashioned Rice Krispie Squares**, omit Mars bars. Melt 10 large marshmallows with butter. Chocolate peanut butter frosting is optional.

YIELD   **25 SQUARES**

MARSHMALLOW BALLS

FOR KIDS OF ALL AGES

½ cup	butter	125 mL
10 oz.	can sweetened condensed milk	300 mL
12 oz.	caramel or toffee, diced	340 g
1 lb.	pkg. marshmallows	454 g
10 cups	Special K cereal	2.5 L

- In a medium saucepan, over low heat, melt butter with milk and caramel. Keep warm.
- One at a time, pierce marshmallows with a fork;, dip in caramel mixture, shaking off excess; roll in cereal. Place cereal-covered marshmallows on parchment-lined cookie sheets. Freeze.
- Place frozen balls in a freezer container. Cover and freeze until needed.

YIELD   **4 DOZEN**

INDEX

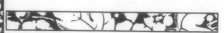

BREADS & MUFFINS

Apple Raisin Muffins	21 (B)
Applesauce Loaf	25 (T)
Baked Croûtons	**58 (K)**
Baking Powder Biscuits	13 (T)
Banana Bread	**11 (K)**
Banana Chocolate Chip Muffins	22 (B)
Banana Gumdrop Loaf	23 (T)
Banana Muffins	**8 (K)**
Blueberry Banana Bread	**11 (K)**
Blueberry Lemon Muffins	**7 (K)**
Blueberry Orange Muffins	18 (T)
Blueberry or Strawberry Muffins	**7 (K)**
Blueberry Yogurt Bran Muffins	24 (B)
Braided Sesame Loaf	**21 (K)**
Bran-Cran Muffins	**8 (K)**
Bran Muffins	17 (T), 23 (B)
Buttermilk Biscuits	**6 (K)**
Buttermilk, Sour Cream or Yogurt Muffins	**7 (K)**
Cheese Biscuits	13 (T)
Cheese Bread	16 (T)
Cheese Bread/Buns	12 (B)
Cheese Corn Muffins	13 (B)
Cheese Corn Sticks	13 (B)
Cherry Triangles	9 (B)
Cinnamon Buns	**16 (K)**
Cornbread	14, 15 (T)
Cranberry Orange Muffins	**7 (K)**
Date Loaf	24 (T)
Dilly Cheese Bread	**22 (K)**
Dumplings	**76 (K)**
Focaccia	**19 (K)**
Garlic Cheddar Loaf	14 (B)
Good Ol' Plain Muffins	**7 (K)**
Herb Biscuits	13 (T)
Herbed Beer Bread	15 (B)
Hot Cross Buns	**18 (K)**
Johnny Cake	14 (T)
Julekake	**15 (K)**
Kolach	13 (B)
Lemon Loaf	24 (T), 175 (B)
Lemon Yogurt Scones	19 (B)
Multi-grain and Sunflower Seed Bread.	**23 (K)**
Multi-grain Muffins	**10 (K)**
Old-Fashioned Nut Bread	18 (B)
Onion and Cheese Bread	14 (B)
Orange Muffins	19 (T)
Overnight Buns	26 (T)
Overnight Cinnamon Pull-Aparts	11 (B)
Overnight Coffee Cake	22 (T)
Panettone	**14 (K)**
Parsley Dumplings	73 (T)
Pecan Banana Bread	**11 (K)**
Pepper Corn Bread	15 (T)
Pumpkin Babka	10 (B)
Rhubarb Muffins	20 (T)
Rhubarb Oat Muffins	**9 (K)**
Rye Bread	**24 (K)**
Sour Cream Coffee Cake	21 (T)
Tea Cake Muffins	20 (B)
Tomato Basil Bread	16 (B)
Traditional French Bread	**20 (K)**
White Bread	8 (B)
Whole-Wheat Bread	6 (B)
Whole-Wheat Bread/Buns	7 (B)
Whole-Wheat Soda Bread	17 (B)
Yorkshire Pudding	12 (T)

BREAKFAST & BRUNCH

"All-In-One" Breakfast	**30 (K)**
Asparagus Ham Bake	**32 (K)**
Baked Apple Pancake	**27 (K)**
Baked Canadian Bacon	8 (T)
Banana Nut French Toast	**29 (K)**
Banana-Chocolate Crêpes	11 (T)
Basic Pancake Batter	9 (T)
Breakfast Bake	7 (T)
Broccoli-Ham Brunch	**35 (K)**
Cheese Soufflé	31 (B)
Cottage Cheese Crêpes	10 (T)
Crustless Quiche	36 (B)
Deluxe Potatoes	107 (B)
Eggs Benedict	30 (B)
French Loaf Pizza	40 (B)
Ham and Cheese Quiche	37 (B)
Hash-Brown Quiche	36 (B)
Mexican Oven-Baked Omelet	35 (B)
Muesli	**26 (K)**
Orange French Toast	8 (T)
Oven-Baked Omelet	6 (T), 35 (B)
Overnight Berry French Toast	**28 (K)**
Pasta with Cool Seafood Sauce	38 (B)
Pizza	39 (B)
Pizza by the Foot	**36 (K)**
Puffy Oven Pancake	**26 (K)**
Salmon Soufflé	32 (B)
Shrimpwiches	**35 (K)**
Spinach Frittata	**31 (K)**
Spinach Mushroom Crêpe Filling	11 (T)
Welsh Rarebit	**30 (K)**
Zucchini Tomato Impossible Pie	35 (B)

COFFEE CAKES

Chocolate Chip Coffee Ring	26 (B)
Orange Coffee Cake	27 (B)
Orange Coffee Cake	27 (B)
Overnight Coffee Cake	22 (T)
Rhubarb Cake	28 (B)
Sour Cream Coffee Cake	21 (T)
Strawberry Streusel Coffee Cake	**12 (K)**
Streusel Coffee Cake	25 (B)
Toffee Apple Coffee Cake	**13 (K)**
Breakfast Bake	7 (T)
Broccoli Bake	54 (T)
Broccoli Carrot Casserole	**100 (K)**
Broccoli-Ham Brunch	**35 (K)**
Broccoli Onion Casserole	100 (B)
Broccoli Salad	81 (B)

Brownie Mousse Dessert	112 (T)
Brown Sugar Sauce	146 (B)
Brown Sugar Shortbread	**185 (K)**
Bruschetta	48 (B)
Buckwheat Casserole	**114 (K)**
Butter Fingers	185 (B)
Butter Icing	184 (T)
Butter Tarts	183 (B)
Buttermilk Biscuits	**6 (K)**
Buttermilk, Sour Cream or Yogurt Muffins	**7 (K)**

C

Cabbage Rolls	55, 75 (T)
Cabbage Soup	63 (B)
Caesar Dressing	78 (B)
Caesar Salad	78 (B)
Cajun Rice	**110 (K)**
Cajun Seasoning	**123 (K)**
Cannelloni	80 (T)
Caramel Frosting	**180 (K)**
Caramel Sauce	135 (T)
Caramel Toffee Squares	179 (B)
Carrot & Potato Steamed Pudding	**162 (K)**
Carrot Apple Salad	**81 (K)**
Carrot Cake	147 (T)
Carrot Copper Penny Salad	30 (T)
Carrot Marmalade	68 (T)
Carrot Orange Salad	**87 (K)**
Carrot Pecan Cake	**173 (K)**
Carrot Pudding	177 (T)
Carrot Salad	30 (T)
Cauliflower Broccoli Salad	**89 (K)**
Cauliflower Casserole	52 (T)
Cauliflower Soup	60 (B)
Cedar Planked Salmon	**117 (K)**
Cheddar Cheese/Potato Pyrohy Filling	106 (T)
Cheddar Scalloped Potatoes	**109 (K)**
Cheese Biscuits	13 (T)
Cheese Bread	16 (T), 12 (B)
Cheesecake – Basic	110 (T)
Cheese Corn Muffins	13 (B)
Cheese Corn Sticks	13 (B)
Cheese Potatoes	106 (B)
Cheese Soufflé	31 (B)
Cherry-Almond Bundt Cake	180 (T)
Cherry-Almond Nanaimo Bars	159 (T)
Cherry Coconut Bars	154 (T)
Cherry Triangles	9 (B)
Chewy Granola Bars	**192 (K)**
Chicken and Egg Noodles	92 (T)
Chicken and Rice	135 (B)
Chicken Cacciatore	**128 (K)**
Chicken Cashew Stir-Fry	128 (B)
Chicken Drumsticks	134 (B)
Chicken Kale Soup	**64 (K)**
Chicken 'n' Trimmings	132 (K)
Chicken Paprika (Paprikas Csirke)	91 (T)
Chicken Pasta Suprême	131 (B)
Chicken Rice Casserole	130 (B)

Lemon Dill Sauce. . . . . 91 (B)
Lemon Garlic Asparagus. . . . . . 98 (B)
Lemon Garlic Marinade. . . . . **145 (K)**
Lemon Glaze . . . . 175 (B)
Lemon Loaf. . . . . 24 (T), 175 (B)
Lemon Meringue Pie . . . . 131 (T)
Lemon Mousse. . . . . 114 (T)
Lemon Poppy Seed Pound
  Cake . . . . **182 (K)**
Lemon Risotto. . . . . **111 (K)**
Lemon Sauce . . . . 122 (T)
Lemon Sauce for Fish. . . . . . . 97 (T)
Lemon Snow . . . . 116 (T)
Lemon Soufflé . . . . 115 (T)
Lemon Squares . . . . 157 (T), 182 (B)
Lemon Yogurt Dressing . . . . . 74 (B)
Lemon Yogurt Scones. . . . . . . 19 (B)
Lentil Sausage Potage. . . . . . . **71 (K)**
Light Fruit Cake. . . . . 178 (T)
Lima Bean-Sausage Casserole . . 89 (T)
Lime Soy Glaze . . . . **131 (K)**
Linguine with Red Clam Sauce 143 (B)
Linguine with Seafood Sauce . 142 (B)
Liqueur Glaze . . . . **182 (K)**
Lumberjack Cake. . . . . **179 (K)**

M
Macaroni & Ham Salad . . . . . . 83 (B)
Macaroni & Salmon Salad . . . . 82 (B)

MAIN COURSES

BEEF
Beef Burger Jelly Roll . . . . . . 117 (B)
Beef Chow Mein Casserole. . 120 (B)
Beef Mushroom Cups. . . . . . 118 (B)
Beef Nacho Casserole . . . . . . 119 (B)
Beef 'n' Broccoli Stir-Fry. . . **133 (K)**
Beef Stew . . . . 72 (T)
Beef Stroganoff. . . . . **138 (K)**
Black Bean Chili . . . . **137 (K)**
Cannelloni . . . . 80 (T)
Chili Con Carne. . . . . 77 (T)
Classic Sauerbraten. . . . . . . **132 (K)**
Ground Beef Loaf. . . . . 76 (T)
Ground Beef Rolls . . . . 75 (T)
Ground Beef Stroganoff . . . . 118 (B)
Hash-Brown Stroganoff Pie. . 74 (T)
Individual Meat Loaves. . . . . 115 (B)
Lasagne. . . . . 81 (T)
Meatballs . . . . 78 (T)
Mexicali Beef Pie . . . . **142 (K)**
Moussaka . . . . **134 (K)**
New England Boiled Dinner. 112 (B)
Old-Fashioned Shepherd's Pie 73 (T)
Pastitsio . . . . **136 (K)**
Pepper Steak. . . . . 71 (T)
Porcupine Meat Balls . . . . . . 116 (B)
Reuben Casserole . . . . 114 (B)
Rouladen . . . . 70 (T)
Shish Kebabs . . . . 113 (B)
Succulent Roast Beef . . . . . **130 (K)**
Tex-Mex Lasagne . . . . **141 (K)**

Tomato Meat Sauce . . . . . . 136 (K)
Zucchini Lasagne . . . . 123 (B)

FISH & SEAFOOD
Baked Codfish . . . . 98 (T)
Baked Snapper. . . . . 98 (T)
Cedar Planked Salmon. . . . . **117 (K)**
Chicken, Sausage & Shrimp
  Jambalaya. . . . . **123 (K)**
Coquille St. Jacques . . . . . . 99 (T)
Crab-Zucchini Casserole. . . . 100 (T)
Fish Fillets in Lemon Sauce. . 97 (T)
Grilled Fish Steaks . . . . 137 (B)
Grilled Walleye. . . . . **116 (K)**
Halibut with Sesame Seeds. . **116 (K)**
Linguine with Red Clam Sauce 143 (B)
Linguine with Seafood Sauce 142 (B)
Marinated Baked Salmon. . . **117 (K)**
Pasta with Cool Seafood Sauce 38 (B)
Pheasant and Rice. . . . . 135 (B)
Salmon Dill Loaf . . . . 138 (B)
Seafood Casserole . . . . 100 (T)
Seafood Lasagne . . . . 144 (B)
Shrimp Jambalaya. . . . . 141 (B)
Smoked Salmon Pâté . . . . . . 166 (T)
Stuffed Fillets of Sole . . . . . 136 (B)
Szechuan Shrimp . . . . **118 (K)**

MEATLESS
Baked Beans. . . . . 102 (T)
Cornmeal Nachynka Casserole 108 (T)
Mushroom Cutlets . . . . 101 (T)
Parsley Dumplings . . . . 73 (T)
Pasta Puttanesca . . . . **152 (K)**
Pyrohy
  Cheddar Cheese/Potato Filling 106 (T)
  Cottage Cheese Pyrohy Filling 107 (T)
  Sauerkraut Pyrohy Filling. . . 107 (T)
Spaghetti Sauce. . . . . 103 (T)

PASTA
Cannelloni . . . . 80 (T)
Chicken and Egg Noodles . . 92 (T)
Chicken Pasta Suprême. . . . . 131 (B)
Gnocchi . . . . 105 (T)
Lasagne. . . . . 81 (T)
Linguine with Red Clam Sauce 143 (B)
Linguine with Seafood Sauce 142 (B)
Parmesan Cheese Sauce with
  Pasta and Vegetables . . . . . 104 (T)
Pasta Carbonara . . . . **151 (K)**
Pasta Perogies. . . . . **150 (K)**
Pasta Puttanesca . . . . **152 (K)**
Pasta with Cool Seafood Sauce 38 (B)
Pastitsio . . . . **136 (K)**
Seafood Lasagne . . . . 144 (B)
Spaghetti Sauce. . . . . 103 (T)
Spinach Lasagne . . . . 81 (T)
Tex-Mex Lasagne . . . . **141 (K)**
Zucchini Lasagne . . . . 123 (B)

PORK
Bean Sausage Hot Pot . . . . **149 (K)**
Chicken, Sausage & Shrimp
  Jambalaya. . . . . **123 (K)**

Chinese Sweet 'n' Sour Ribs . 87 (T)
Cranberry Sausage Dressing **129 (K)**
Glazed Ham. . . . . 169 (T)
Honey Pork Chops. . . . . 84 (T)
Jamaican Pork. . . . . 125 (B)
Lima Bean-Sausage Casserole 89 (T)
Marinated Pork Roast . . . . . . 83 (T)
Orange-Marinated
  Barbecued Pork . . . . **147 (K)**
Pasta Carbonara . . . . **151 (K)**
Pasta Perogies. . . . . **150 (K)**
Pepper Steak. . . . . 71 (T)
Polish Hunter's Stew (*Bigos*) **148 (K)**
Pork Chops à la Orange . . . **146 (K)**
Pork Chops and Rice . . . . . . 85 (T)
Pork Loin Roast with Peach
  Sauce . . . . **146 (K)**
Pork Satay . . . . **145 (K)**
Potato-Ham Scallop . . . . 88 (T)
Spareribs in Sauce. . . . . 86 (T)
Stuffed Pork Roast . . . . 124 (B)
Stuffed Spareribs. . . . . 127 (B)
Sweet and Spicy Pork . . . . . 126 (B)
Tourtière. . . . . 163 (T)

POULTRY
Barbecued Chicken . . . . 95 (T)
Chicken and Egg Noodles . . 92 (T)
Chicken and Rice. . . . . 135 (B)
Chicken Cacciatore. . . . . . . **128 (K)**
Chicken Cashew Stir-Fry . . . 128 (B)
Chicken Drumsticks. . . . . . . 134 (B)
Chicken 'n' Trimmings . . . . . 132 (B)
Chicken Paprika . . . . 91 (T)
Chicken Pasta Suprême. . . . . 131 (B)
Chicken Rice Casserole. . . . . 130 (B)
Chicken, Sausage & Shrimp
  Jambalaya. . . . . **123 (K)**
Chicken-Spinach Casserole. . 94 (T)
Chicken Wings. . . . . 96 (T)
Coq au Vin . . . . **119 (K)**
Cranberry Chicken. . . . . 93 (T)
Cranberry Sausage Dressing **129 (K)**
Crispy Oven Chicken . . . . . **127 (K)**
Curried Chicken Thighs. . . . **125 (K)**
Garlicky Sticky Chicken
  Thighs/Wings. . . . . **126 (K)**
Greek Lemon Chicken
  with Potatoes . . . . **124 (K)**
Mediterranean Apricot &
  Olive Chicken. . . . . **120 (K)**
One-Dish Chicken and Rice. 130 (B)
Poulet de la France . . . . 129 (B)
Roast Turkey. . . . . 170 (T)
Stuffed Chicken Breasts . . . . 90 (T)
Thai Thighs . . . . 133 (B)
Turkey à la King. . . . . 174 (T)
Turkey Dressing . . . . 171 (T)
Turkey Soup . . . . 173 (T)
Turkey Stock. . . . . 172 (T)

STEWS

Beef Stew . . . . 72 (T)
Dumplings . . . . 73 (T), **76 (K)**
"Gone-All-Day" Stew . . . . . **73 (K)**
Hot Tornado Stew . . . . **74 (K)**
Irish Lamb Stew . . . . **76 (K)**
Polish Hunter's Stew *(Bigos)* **148 (K)**
Pork Ragoût with Sweet
  Potatoes and Apricots . . . . **72 (K)**
Sweet 'n' Sour Stew . . . . . . **75 (K)**

VEAL

Cannelloni . . . . 80 (T)
Osso Buco . . . . **143 (K)**
Veal Cordon Blue . . . . 82 (T)
Veal Parmigiana . . . . **144 (K)**
Mango Salsa Jelly . . . . **45 (K)**
Mango Tomato Fresh Salsa . . . **45 (K)**
Manhattan Clam Chowder . . . . 66 (B)
Maple Ham and Mushroom
  Wild Rice . . . . **113 (K)**
Maple Sugar Pie . . . . 183 (T)
Marinated Baked Salmon . . . . **117 (K)**
Marinated Onions . . . . 80 (B)
Marinated Pork Roast . . . . 83 (T)
Marinating Dry Rub . . . . **117 (K)**
Marshmallow Balls . . . . **196 (K)**
Marshmallow Raspberry Swirl . 154 (B)
Mascarpone Filling . . . . **168 (K)**
Mascarpone Strawberry
  Cheesecake . . . . **168 (K)**
Matrimonial Squares . . . . 156 (T)
Meatballs . . . . 78 (T)
Mediterranean Apricot &
  Olive Chicken . . . . **120 (K)**
Melon and Chicken Salad . . . . 74 (B)
Meringue . . . . 131, 132 (T),
                      161 (B), **166 (K)**
Mexicali Beef Pie . . . . **142 (K)**
Mexican Layered Dip . . . . **43 (K)**
Mexican Oven-Baked Omelet . 35 (B)
Mexican Rice Casserole . . . . . . 110 (B)
Mexican Wedding Cake . . . . . . 141 (T)
Minestrone . . . . 67 (B)
Mini Cheesecakes . . . . 149 (B)
Mini Chocolate Cheesecakes . . 149 (B)
Miracle Soup . . . . 72 (B)
Mixed Vegetable Casserole . . . . 102 (B)
Mocha Cake . . . . **177 (K)**
Mocha Coffee Mix . . . . 58 (B)
Moussaka . . . . **134 (K)**
Muesli . . . . **26 (K)**
Multi-grain and Sunflower
  Seed Bread . . . . **23 (K)**
Multi-grain Muffins . . . . **10 (K)**
Mushroom Cutlets . . . . 101 (T)
Mushroom Sauce . . . . 40 (T)
Mushrooms & Peppers . . . . . **88 (K)**
Mushrooms with Brazil Nut
  Stuffing . . . . **50 (K)**

N

Nanaimo Bars . . . . 159 (T)
New England Boiled Dinner . . 112 (B)
Niçoise Tuna, Shrimp, Crab or
  Lobster Filling . . . . **39 (K)**
Noodles . . . . 92 (T)

O

Oatmeal Chocolate Chip Cookies 152 (T)
Oatmeal Coconut Cookies . . . . 153 (T)
Oatmeal Raisin Spice Cake . . **180 (K)**
Oil & Garlic Croutons . . . . . . **58 (K)**
Old-Fashioned Nut Bread . . . . 18 (B)
Old-Fashioned Rice Krispie
  Squares . . . . **196 (K)**
Old-Fashioned Shepherd's Pie . . 73 (T)
Old-Fashioned Walnut Squares . 181 (B)
One-Dish Chicken and Rice . . 130 (B)
Onion and Cheese Bread . . . . . 14 (B)
Onion Cucumber Salad . . . . . **88 (K)**
Onion Sauce for Meatballs . . . . 79 (T)
Oobleck . . . . 202 (B)
Orange Almond Lettuce Salad **83 (K)**
Orange Chiffon Cake . . . . 165 (B)
Orange Coffee Cake . . . . 27 (B)
Orange Cream Cheese Frosting . 166 (B)
Orange French Toast . . . . 8 (T)
Orange Glaze . . . . 172 (B)
Orange Loaves . . . . 175 (B)
Orange-Marinated Barbecued
  Pork . . . . **147 (K)**
Orange Muffins . . . . 19 (T)
Orange Onion Salad . . . . **87 (K)**
Orange Pineapple Cake . . . . . . 174 (B)
Orange Rum Cake . . . . 172 (B)
Orange Sauce . . . . **163 (K)**
Oreo Cookies . . . . 199 (B)
Oriental Hot and Sour Soup . . 71 (T)
Orzo, Barley & Mushrooms . . **114 (K)**
Osso Buco (Braised Veal
  Shanks) . . . . **143 (K)**
Oven-Baked Bacon Cheddar
  Potatoes . . . . **108 (K)**
Oven-Baked Omelet . . . . . 6 (T), 35 (B)
Overnight Berry French Toast **28 (K)**
Overnight Buns . . . . 26 (T)
Overnight Cinnamon Pull-Aparts 11 (B)
Overnight Coffee Cake . . . . 22 (T)

P

Pancake Batter . . . . 9 (T)
Panettone . . . . **14 (K)**
Parmesan Cheese Sauce with
  Pasta and Vegetables . . . . 104 (T)
Parmesan Garlic Croûtons . . . **58 (K)**
Parsley Dumplings . . . . 73 (T)
Pasta and Fresh Vegetable Salad 92 (K)
Pasta Carbonara . . . . **151 (K)**
Pasta Perfection . . . . **93 (K)**
Pasta Perogies . . . . **150 (K)**
Pasta Puttanesca . . . . **152 (K)**
Pasta with Cool Seafood Sauce . 38 (B)

Pastitsio . . . . **136 (K)**
Pavlova . . . . 147 (B)
Peanut Butter Cones . . . . 190 (B)
Peanut Butter Cookies 151 (T), 199 (B)
Peanut Butter Nanaimo Bars . . 159 (T)
Peanut Ginger Sauce . . . . 133 (B)
Pears in Brown Sugar Sauce . . . 146 (B)
Pecan Banana Bread . . . . **11 (K)**
Pecan Butter Tart Squares . . . . . 182 (T)
Pecan Crescents . . . . 184 (T)
Pecan Praline Tart . . . . **167 (K)**
People Chow . . . . 194 (B)
Pepper Corn Bread . . . . 15 (T)
Pepper Steak . . . . 71 (T)
Peppery Cheese Melts . . . . 54 (B)
Pheasant and Rice . . . . 135 (B)
Pie Pastry . . . . 133 (T)
Pimiento Pickle Filling . . . . . **38 (K)**
Piña Colada Dessert . . . . 173 (B)
Pineapple Aloha Pie . . . . 156 (B)
Pineapple Bean Pot . . . . 106 (B)
Pineapple Dessert . . . . 117 (T)
Pineapple Sauce for Meatballs . . 79 (T)
Pineapple Upside-Down Cake . 136 (B)
Pistachio Cake . . . . 174 (B)
Pizza . . . . 39 (B)
Pizza by the Foot . . . . **36 (K)**
Pizza Soup . . . . 66 (B)
Playdough . . . . 201 (B)
Polish Hunter's Stew *(Bigos)* . . **148 (K)**
Popcorn Balls . . . . 195 (B)
Poppy Seed Chiffon Cake . . . . . 165 (B)
Poppy Seed Dressing . . . 75 (B), **92 (K)**
Poppy Seed Lemon Cake . . . . . 138 (T)
Porcupine Meat Balls . . . . 116 (T)
Pork Chops à la Orange . . . . . **146 (K)**
Pork Chops and Rice . . . . 85 (T)
Pork Loin Roast with Peach
  Sauce . . . . **146 (K)**
Pork Ragoût with Sweet Potatoes
  and Apricots . . . . **72 (K)**
Pork Satay . . . . **145 (K)**
Potato-Cheese Soup . . . . 47 (T)
Potato-Ham Scallop . . . . 88 (T)
Potato Pancakes . . . . 58 (T)
Potato Patties . . . . 57 (T)
Potato Salad . . . . 28 (T)
Poulet de la France . . . . 129 (B)
Pound Cake . . . . **182 (K)**

PRESERVES & PICKLES

Already Cut Pickles . . . . 66 (T)
Antipasto . . . . 63 (T)
Apple Chutney . . . . . **95 (K)**, 96 (B)
Beet Pickles . . . . 68 (T)
Beet Pickles in a Pail . . . . . . **96 (K)**
Bread and Butter Pickles . . . . 65 (T)
Carrot Marmalade . . . . 68 (T)
Christmas Pepper Jelly . . . . . . 164 (T)
Dill Pickles . . . . 64 (T)
English Mincemeat . . . . 175 (T)
Green Tomato Mincemeat . . . 176 (T)

Tomato Basil Bread . . . . 16 (B)
Tomato Bocconcini Salad . . . . 80 (B)
Tomato Meat Sauce . . . . **136 (K)**
Tomato Mozzarella Salad . . . . 80 (B)
Tomato Sauce . . . . 62 (T)
Tomato Soup Spice Cake . . . . 164 (B)
Tortellini Spinach Soup . . . . . **60 (K)**
Tourtière . . . . 163 (T)
Traditional French Bread . . . . **20 (K)**
Triple Chocolate Cake . . . . . . 170 (B)
Turkey à la King . . . . 174 (T)
Turkey Barley Soup . . . . **66 (K)**
Turkey Dressing . . . . 171 (T)
Turkey – Roast . . . . 170 (T)
Turkey Soup . . . . 173 (T)
Turkey Stock . . . . 172 (T)
Turnip Carrot Puff . . . . 103 (B)
Turnip Casserole . . . . 57 (T)
Turtle Cake . . . . 169 (B)
Twenty-Four hour Barbecue
  Coleslaw . . . . **94 (K)**
Twenty-Four Hour Fruit Salad . 36 (T)
Twice-Baked Potatoes . . . . . . **108 (K)**
Two-Week Coleslaw . . . . 34 (T)

V

Vanilla Cream Filling . . . . . . **164 (K)**
Vanilla Cream Topping . . . . . **169 (K)**
Vanilla Crumb Crust . . . . 156 (B)
Vanilla Glaze . . . . **17 (K)**, 27 (B)
Vanilla or Chocolate Crumb
  Crust . . . . 156 (B)
Vanilla Sauce . . . . **172 (K)**
Veal Cordon Bleu . . . . 82 (T)
Veal Parmigiana . . . . **144 (K)**

VEGETABLES

Baked Beans . . . . 102 (T)
Baked Sweet Potato . . . . 169 (T)
Bean Casserole . . . . 105 (B)
Beet Leaf Rolls . . . . 55 (T)
Blue Cheese Broiled Tomatoes 99 (K)
Broccoli Bake . . . . 54 (T)
Broccoli Carrot Casserole . . **100 (K)**
Broccoli Onion Casserole . . . . 100 (B)
Cabbage Rolls . . . . 55 (T)
Cauliflower Casserole . . . . . . 52 (T)
Cheddar Scalloped Potatoes. 109 (K)
Cheese Potatoes . . . . 106 (B)
Corn/Pepper Casserole . . . . . . 100 (B)
Cornmeal Nachynka Casserole 108 (T)
Creamed Carrots . . . . 53 (T)
Creole Lima Beans . . . . 104 (B)
Deluxe Potatoes . . . . 107 (B)
Deviled Corn . . . . **105 (K)**
Fried Green Tomatoes . . . . . **98 (K)**
Garlicky Cherry Tomatoes . . **98 (K)**
German-Style Cabbage Rolls . 109 (B)
Glazed Onions . . . . 56 (T)
Glazed Vegetables . . . . 101 (B)
Gnocchi . . . . 105 (T)
Green Bean Casserole . . . . . **101 (K)**

Harvard Beets . . . . **106 (K)**
Irish Potatoes . . . . 108 (B)
Lazy Cabbage Rolls . . . . 109 (B)
Lemon Garlic Asparagus . . . . 98 (B)
Lima Bean-Sausage Casserole . 89 (T)
Mexican Rice Casserole . . . . . 110 (B)
Mixed Vegetable Casserole . . . 102 (B)
Mushroom Cutlets . . . . 101 (T)
Oven-Baked Bacon Cheddar
  Potatoes . . . . **108 (K)**
Parmesan Cheese Sauce with
  Pasta and Vegetables . . . . . 104 (T)
Pasta Puttanesca . . . . **152 (K)**
Pineapple Bean Pot . . . . 106 (B)
Potato Pancakes . . . . 58 (T)
Potato Patties . . . . 57 (T)
Pyrohy . . . . 106 (T)
Ratatouille Stir-Fry . . . . **99 (K)**
Red Cabbage with Apples . . . 54 (T)
Roasted Garlic . . . . **107 (K)**
Roasted Root Vegetable
  Medley . . . . **106 (K)**
Scalloped Mushrooms . . . . . . 98 (B)
Six Bean Mix . . . . **149 (K)**
Spaghetti Sauce . . . . 103 (T)
Spinach Bake . . . . 99 (B)
Spinach Balls . . . . 99 (B)
Stuffed Tomatoes . . . . 60 (T)
Sunny Day Carrots . . . . **100 (K)**
Tender-Crisp Chinese
  Vegetables . . . . **102 (K)**
Turnip Carrot Puff . . . . 103 (B)
Turnip Casserole . . . . 57 (T)
Twice-Baked Potatoes . . . . . **108 (K)**
Vegetarian Moussaka . . . . . . **135 (K)**
Zucchini Pancakes . . . . 59 (T)
Zucchini Tomato Stir-Fry . . . . 59 (T)
Vegetarian Moussaka . . . . . . **135 (K)**
Vienna Coffee Mix . . . . 58 (B)

W

Waldorf Salad . . . . 35 (T)
Walnut Slice . . . . **195 (K)**
Wartime Christmas Cake . . . . . 179 (T)
Welsh Rarebit . . . . **30 (K)**
Wheat Berry Caviar . . . . **41 (K)**
Wheat Salad . . . . 85 (B)
White Batter Cake . . . . **170 (K)**
White Bread . . . . 8 (B)
White Cake . . . . 137 (T)
Whole-Wheat Bread . . . . . 6 (B), 7 (B)
Whole-Wheat Soda Bread . . . . 17 (B)
Wilted Spinach Salad . . . . . . **82 (K)**
Wonton Soup . . . . 44 (T)
Wontons . . . . 44 (T)

Y

Yellow Batter Cake . . . . **170 (K)**
Yogurt Banana Dressing . . . . **81 (K)**
Yogurt Herb Dressing . . . . 90 (B)
Yogurt Pecan Drop Cookies . . **186 (K)**
Yorkshire Pudding . . . . 12 (T)

YOUNGER COOKS

Almond Roca . . . . 198 (B)
Crispy Nibblers . . . . 194 (B)
"Dirt" Dessert . . . . 196 (B)
Eatmore Bars . . . . 198 (B)
Finger Jellies . . . . 201 (B)
Hallowe'en Cookies . . . . 199 (B)
Jellied Yogurt . . . . 200 (B)
Oobleck . . . . 202 (B)
Oreo Cookies . . . . 199 (B)
Peanut Butter Cones . . . . 190 (B)
Peanut Butter Cookies . . . . . . 199 (B)
People Chow . . . . 194 (B)
Playdough . . . . 201 (B)
Popcorn Balls . . . . 195 (B)
St. Patrick's Day Cookies . . . . 199 (B)
Slab Cookies . . . . 200 (B)
Snackin' Crackers . . . . 193 (B)
Special K Squares . . . . 197 (B)
Yummy Yam Squares . . . . **193 (K)**

Z

Zesty Chili Filling for
  Deviled Eggs . . . . **38 (K)**
Zucchini Cake . . . . 147 (T)
Zucchini Chocolate Cake . . . . . 145 (T)
Zucchini Lasagne . . . . 123 (B)
Zucchini Pancakes . . . . 59 (T)
Zucchini Tomato Impossible Pie 35 (B)
Zucchini Tomato Stir-Fry . . . . . 59 (T)